GW00732875

San Francisco

Chief Editor	Cynthia Clayton Ochterbeck
Senior Editor	M. Linda Lee
Contributing Writers	Shea Dean, M. Linda Lee, Megan Thompson
Production Coordinator	Allison M. Simpson
Cartography	Peter Wrenn
Photo Editor	Brigitta L. House
Documentation	Megan Thompson
Production	Octavo Design and Production
	Apopka, Florida
Cover Design	Paris Venise Design
	Paris, 17e
Printing and Binding	Quebecor World
	Laval, Québec

Michelin North America
One Parkway South
Greenville, SC 29615
USA
800-423-0485
www.michelin-us.com
email: TheGreenGuide-us@us.michelin.com

Special Sales:

For information regarding bulk sales, customized editions and premium sales, please contact our Customer Service Departments:

USA – 800-423-0485   **Canada** – 800-361-8236

Manufacture française des pneumatiques Michelin
Société en commandite par actions au capital de 304 000 000 EUR
Place des Carmes-Déchaux – 63 Clermont-Ferrand (France)
R.C.S. Clermont-FD B 855 800 507

Note to the reader:

While every effort is made to ensure that all information in this guide is correct and up-to-date, Michelin Travel Publications (Michelin North America, Inc.) accepts no liability for any direct, indirect or consequential losses howsoever caused so far as such can be excluded by law.

Admission prices listed for sights in this guide are for a single adult, unless otherwise specified.

Table of Contents

Table of Contents

THE MICHELIN STARS

For more than 75 years, travelers have used the Michelin stars to take the guesswork out of planning a trip. Our star-rating system helps you make the best decision on where to go, what to do, and what to see. A three-star rating means it's one of the "absolutelys"; two stars means it's one of the "should sees"; and one star says it's one of the "sees" – a must if you have the time.

★★★	Absolutely Must See
★★	Really Must See
★	Must See

Three-Star Sights★★★

Alcatraz★★★
Asian Art Museum★★★
Chinatown★★★
Coit Tower★★★
Conzelman Road★★★
Fisherman's Wharf★★★
Golden Gate Bridge★★★
Golden Gate Park★★★
Lombard Street★★★
Muir Woods NM★★★
Napa Valley★★★
Postcard Row★★★
San Carlos Borromeo de Carmelo Mission★★★
Twin Peaks★★★
Wine Country★★★

Two-Star Sights★★

Angel Island
  State Park★★
Bank of America Center★★
Bank of California★★
Bay Bridge★★
Berkeley★★
Cable Car Museum★★
California Academy
  of Sciences★★
California Palace
  of the Legion of Honor★★
Carmel★★
City Hall★★
The Cannery★★
COPIA★★
di Rosa Preserve★★

Don Clausen
  Fish Hatchery★★
Eugene O'Neill NHS★★
Exploratorium★★
Fairmont Hotel★★
Ferry Building★★
Filbert Steps★★
Financial District★★
First Interstate Center★★
Fort Ross SHP★★
Ghirardelli Square★★
Golden Gate NRA★★
Grant Avenue★★
Haas-Lilienthal House★★
Hallidie Building★★
Hyde Street Pier★★

Jack London SHP★★
Jackson Square★★
Japanese Tea Garden★★
M. H. de Young
    Memorial Museum★★
Marin Headlands★★
Mendocino★★
Mendocino Headlands SP★★
Monterey★★
Monterey Bay Aquarium★★
Mount Tamalpais SP★★
Natural History Museum★★
Nob Hill★★
North Beach★★
Oakland Museum
    of California★★

Pacific Heights★★
Palace Hotel★★
Palace of Fine Arts★★
Paramount Theatre★★
Petaluma Adobe SHP★★
Point Lobos
    State Reserve★★
Point Reyes
    National Seashore★★
The Presidio★★
Rooftop at
    Yerba Buena Gardens★★
St. Francis Hotel★★
SBC Park★★
San Francisco War Memorial
    & Performing Arts Center★★
Stinson Beach★★

One-Star Sights ★

Aquarium of the Bay★
Blackhawk Museum★
Civic Center★
Cliff House★
Coastal Defense Batteries★
Conservatory of Flowers★
Curran Theatre★
East Bay Area
Embarcadero Center★
Fort Mason Center★
Fort Point NHS★
Geary Theater★
Grace Cathedral★
Haight Ashbury★
John Muir NHS★
Metreon★
Mission District★
Mission Dolores★
Morrison Planetarium★
National Maritime Museum★
Oakland★
Octagon House★
Pier 39★
Russian Hill★
Saints Peter & Paul Church★
San Francisco Art Institute★

San Francisco National
    Military Cemetery★
San Francisco
    Public Library★
San Francisco Zoo★
Sausalito★
South of Market★
Steinhart Aquarium★
Sutro Bath Ruins★
Wells Fargo
    History Museum★
Yerba-Buena Center
    for the Arts★
Zeum★

The following abbreviations appear in this list: NHS National Historic Site; NM National Monument; NRA National Recreation Area; SHP State Historic Park; SP State Park.

Calendar of Events

Listed below is a selection of San Francisco's most popular annual events. Please note that dates may change from year to year. For more detailed information, contact the San Francisco Convention and Visitors Bureau *(415-391-2000; www.sfvisitor.org)*.

January

Chinese New Year Parade & Celebration 415-982-3000
Chinatown   www.chineseparade.com

Dr. Martin Luther King Jr.'s Birthday   510-268-3777
   Celebration
Bill Graham Civic Auditorium & Yerba Buena Gardens

San Francisco International Art Exposition 877-734-2399
Fort Mason Center   www.sfiae.com

February

Annual Valentine's Day Sex Tour   415-753-7165
San Francisco Zoo

Festival of Winter Classical Concerts   405-968-2213
Robert Mondavi Winery,
   Napa Valley   www.robertmondaviwinery.com

March

NAATA'S San Francisco International
   Asian American Film Festival   415-863-0814, ext. 110
Castro Theatre and Kabuki Theatre   www.naatanet.org

St. Patrick's Day Parade   415-675-9885
Embarcadero to Civic Center

April

Cherry Blossom Festival   415-922-9300
Civic Center & Japantown

Easter Parade & Spring Celebration   415-456-6455
Union St. between Gough
   & Fillmore Sts.   www.sresproductions.com

San Francisco International Film Festival 415-561-5000
Various locations   www.sffs.org

May

Bay to Breakers Race   415-359-2800
Embarcadero to Great Highway   www.carnavalsf.com

Cinco de Mayo Festival   415-826-1401
Mission District

Yerba Buena Gardens Festival   415-543-1718
Yerba Buena Gardens   www.ybgf.org

June

Lesbian/ Gay/Bisexual/Transgender   415-864-3733
   Pride Celebration
Castro District   www.sfpride.org

Calendar of Events

North Beach Festival   415-989-2220
Grant Ave. & Green St.   www.sfnorthbeach.org

Union Street Arts Festival   550-232-5030
Union St. between
    Gough & Steiner Sts.   www.unionstreetfestival.com

July

Fourth of July Waterfront Festival   415-705-5500
Fisherman's Wharf   www.pier39.com

Midsummer Mozart Festival   415-292-9620
Legion of Honor   www.midsummermozart.org

San Francisco Shakespeare Festival 415-865-4434
Golden Gate Park (July–Oct)   www.sfshakes.org

August

AfroSolo Arts Festival   415-771-2376
Yerba Buena Center for the Arts   www.afrosolo.org

Nihonmachi Street Fair   415-771-9861
Japantown & Japan Center   www.nihonmachistreetfair.org

September

Autumn Moon Festival   415-982-6306
Chinatown   www.moonfestival.org

Ghirardelli Chocolate Festival   415-775-5500
Ghirardelli Square   www.ghirardellisq.com

San Francisco Fringe Festival   415-931-1094
Theater District   www.sffringe.org

Sausalito Art Festival   415-331-3757
Marinship Park   www.sausalitoartfestival.org

October

Cable Car Bell-Ringing Championship 415-934-3900
Union Square   www.sfmuni.com

Fleet Week   415-979-4000
Embarcadero & Fisherman's Wharf   www.fleetweek.us

Italian Heritage Parade & Festival   415-986-4036
North Beach   www.sfcolumbusday.org

San Francisco Jazz Festival   415-788-7353
Various locations   www.sfjazz.org

November

Embarcadero Center Building   800-733-6318
    Lighting Ceremony   Justin Herman Plaza

Film Arts Festival of Independent Cinema 415-552-8760
Castro & Roxie theaters   www.filmarts.org

December

Festival of Lights   415-956-3493
Fisherman's Wharf   www.fishermanswharf.org

MICHELIN MUST SEES   **9**

Must Know: Practical Information

Area Codes:
To call between different area codes, dial 1 + area code + seven-digit number. The area code is not necessary for a local call.

San Francisco and Marin County: **415**
Napa Valley and Wine Country: **707**
Berkeley, East Bay, Oakland: **510**

PLANNING YOUR TRIP
Before you go, contact the following agencies to obtain maps and information about sightseeing, accommodations, travel packages, recreational opportunities and seasonal events.

San Francisco Convention & Visitors Bureau
900 Market St., San Francisco, CA 94142
415-391-2000; www.sfvisitor.org

Visitors Information Center
Located on the lower level of Hallidie Plaza
Market & Powell Sts.
Open Mon–Fri 9am–5:30pm,
Sat 9am–3pm, Sun 10am–2pm
415-391-2000

Berkeley Convention & Visitors Bureau
2015 Center St., Berkeley, CA 94704
510-549-7040; www.berkeleycvb.com

Marin County Convention & Visitors Bureau
1013 Larkspur Landing Circle, Larkspur, CA 94939
415-499-5000; www.visitmarin.org

Napa Valley Conference & Visitors Bureau
1310 Napa Town Center, Napa, CA 94559
707-226-7459; www.napavalley.org

Oakland Convention & Visitors Bureau
475 14th St., Suite 120, Oakland, CA 94612
510-839-9000; www.oaklandcvb.com

San Mateo County Convention & Visitors Bureau
111 Anza Blvd., Suite 410, Burlingame, CA 94010
650-348-7600; www.sanmateocountycvb.com

Santa Rosa Convention & Visitors Bureau
9 Fourth St., Santa Rosa, CA 94501
707-577-8674; www.visitsantarosa.com

In the News
San Francisco's two main daily newspapers are the *San Francisco Chronicle (morning; www.sfchron.com)* and the *San Francisco Examiner (afternoon; www.examiner.com)*. The Sunday edition, the *Chronicle-Examiner*, is published jointly and features an extensive arts-and-entertainment supplement. Two weekly alternative papers, *The San Francisco Bay Guardian (www.sfbg.com)* and the *SF Weekly (www.sfweekly.com)*, both published on Wednesday, offer different perspectives of the city as well as diverse and comprehensive entertainment sections.

CityPass – Consider buying a CityPass booklet *($36, adults; $28 ages 5–17; good for 7 consecutive days)*, which gives you substantially discounted admission to the following attractions: Blue & Gold Fleet cruises, San Francisco Museum of Modern Art, Exploratorium, Legion of Honor, and the California Academy of Sciences and Steinhart Aquarium. Booklets also include a 7-day pass for MUNI public transportation and cable cars. Buy your CityPass at the Visitor Information Center *(above)*, at any of the participating attractions, or online at www.citypass.com.

TIPS FOR SPECIAL VISITORS

Disabled Travelers – Federal law requires that businesses (including hotels and restaurants) provide access for the disabled, devices for the hearing impaired, and designated parking spaces. For further information, contact the Society for Accessible Travel and Hospitality (SATH), 347 Fifth Ave., Suite 610, New York NY 10016 *(212-447-7284; www.sath.org)*.

All national parks have facilities for the disabled, and offer free or discounted passes. For details, contact the National Park Service *(Office of Public Inquiries, P.O. Box 37127, Room 1013, Washington DC 20013-7127; 202-208-4747; www.nps.gov)*.

Passengers who will need assistance with train or bus travel should give advance notice to Amtrak *(800-872-7245 or 800-523-6590/TDD; www.amtrak.com)* or Greyhound *(800-752-4841 or 800-345-3109/TDD; www.greyhound.com)*. Reservations for hand-controlled rental cars should be made in advance with the rental company.

Web Sites

Here are some additional Web sites to help you plan your trip:
www.sfgate.com
www.sfguide.com
www.sanfranciscoonline.com

Local Lowdown – The following publications provide detailed information about access for the disabled in San Francisco and Northern California:

• *Access Northern California (ANC, 1427 Grant St., Berkeley, CA 94703; 510-524-2026; www.accessnca.com)*.

• *Access San Francisco (San Francisco Convention & Visitors Bureau; 415-391-2000 or 415-392-0328 TDD; www.sfvisitor.org)*. If you're in town, pick up a copy of this publication at the Visitors Information Center located on the lower level of Hallidie Plaza *(Market & Powell Sts.)*.

• MUNI Access Guide *(San Francisco Municipal Railway; 415-923-6142; TTY 415-351-3443; www.sfmuni.com)*.

Senior Citizens – Many hotels, attractions and restaurants offer discounts to visitors age 62 or older (proof of age may be required). The **American Association of Retired Persons** (AARP), *(601 E St. NW, Washington DC 20049; 202-424-3410; www.aarp.com)* offers discounts to its members.

Important Numbers	
Emergency (Police/Ambulance/Fire Department, 24hrs)	**911**
Police *(non-emergency, Mon–Fri 9am–6pm)*	415-553-0123
Poison Control	800-876-4766
Medical Referral:	
Travelers Medical Group (24hrs)	415-981-1102
SF On-Cal	415-732-7029
Downtown Medical Travel Group	415-862-7177
Visitors Medical Services	415-535-6000
Dental Emergencies	415-421-1435
24-hour Pharmacies: Walgreens (800-289-2273)	
3201 Divisadero St., Marina District	415-931-6415
498 Castro St., Castro District	415-861-6276
Bay Area Transit Information Hotline: (within San Francisco)	**511**
(outside San Francisco)	510-817-1717

WHEN TO GO

Sure, you've heard Mark Twain's jibe that the coldest winter he ever spent was a summer in San Francisco. Even so, the Bay Area enjoys a temperate climate year-round. Although temperatures vary little from season to season, weather conditions can change quite suddenly in the course of a day, and from area to area. Inland temperatures are generally higher than those along the windy oceanfront and the bay shore.

The region's glorious views are at their finest during the clear days of autumn, when daytime temperatures in the 70s make for great sightseeing. Rain is the norm during the winter months with 80 percent of the annual precipitation occurring between November and April, when temperatures hover between 45° and 60°F. The busiest tourist season is July and August; make advance reservations whenever possible and expect long lines for the more popular attractions.

Fog

It may roll in on little cat's feet, but San Francisco's fog can put a damper on your sightseeing—especially if you were planning on enjoying long-range views. When the fog sets in, temperatures drop suddenly, making a sweater or jacket necessary. Spring fogs occur in the early morning and generally lift by mid-day. In summer, fog can last all day by the coast, though it may burn off over inland areas before it comes back in the evening. Autumn days are relatively fog-free. Winter fogs usually occur inland, leaving coastal areas in the clear.

Seasonal Temperatures in San Francisco
(recorded at San Francisco International Airport)

	Jan	Apr	July	Oct
Avg. high	56°F / 13°C	63°F / 17°C	71°F / 21°C	70°F / 21°C
Avg. low	41°F / 5°C	47°F / 8°C	53°F / 12°C	51°F /10°C

GETTING THERE

By Air – San Francisco is served by two international airports:

San Francisco International Airport (SFO) – 13.5mi south of San Francisco via US-101 *(650-821-8211; www.flysfo.com)*.

Oakland International Airport (OAK) – 18mi east of San Francisco via I-80 and I-880 *(510-563-3300; www.flyoakland.com)*.

By Train – Emeryville is the home of the closest railroad station to San Francisco. Located across the bay, the station offers Amtrak and shuttling services *(5885 Landregan St.; 800-872-7245; www.amtrak.com)*.

By Bus – San Francisco's main bus terminal is located at 425 Mission Transbay Station *(415-495-1555)*. For fares, schedules and routes, call 800-231-2222 or visit www.greyhound.com.

SFO's AirTrain

In spring 2003, San Francisco International Airport debuted its AirTrain people mover. This rail system comprises two independent loops that circle the airport, providing travelers with easy access to remote terminals, parking lots, car-rental facilities and the new BART station.

By Car – San Francisco can be easily accessed from a number of major highways. I-280 enters the city from the south. I-80 crosses the Bay Bridge from Berkeley and Oakland *($2 toll for westbound traffic only)*. US-101, which enters San Francisco from the south, also provides access to the city from the north, crossing the Golden Gate Bridge *($5 toll for southbound traffic only)*.

Car Rental Company	Reservations	Internet
Alamo	800-462-5266	www.alamo.com
Avis	800-230-4898	www.avis.com
Budget	800-527-0700	www.drivebudget.com
Dollar	800-800-4000	www.dollar.com
Enterprise	800-736-8222	www.enterprise.com
Hertz	800-654-3131	www.hertz.com
National	800-227-7368	www.nationalcar.com
Thrifty	800-847-4389	www.thrifty.com

GETTING AROUND

By Car – Driving can be a hassle in San Francisco, where the roads are congested and parking is difficult to find and often expensive. Visitors are encouraged not to drive during commuter rush hours (weekdays 7:30am-9am and 4pm-6pm). Cars are, however, useful for visiting surrounding areas such as the Wine Country and Marin County. Use of seat belts is required. Child safety seats are mandatory for children under 6 years and 60 pounds.

Parking – San Francisco's hills pose a special problem when you're parking. When parking on a hill, be sure to turn the front wheels of your vehicle against the curb. Facing downhill, turn the wheels toward the curb; facing uphill, turn the wheels away from the curb. Needless, to say, the use of a parking brake is mandatory.

By Foot – Walking is one of the best ways to explore San Francisco—and a great way to get a workout. The city's Convention and Visitors Bureau lists a variety of walking tours on its Web site *(www.sfvisitor.org)*. If you're planning to walk, it helps to know which streets are the steepest *(see list in Landmarks/Lombard Street)*.

By Public Transportation – The **San Francisco Municipal Railway (MUNI)** operates an extensive network of transportation lines using diesel and electric buses, light-rail streetcars and cable cars *(415-673-6864; www.sfmuni.com)*. Golden Gate Transit *(415-923-2000; www.goldengatetransit.org)* provides bus services to Marin, Contro Costa and Sonoma Counties; SamTrans *(650-508-6455; www.samtrans.com)* serves San Mateo County; and AC Transit *(510-817-1717; www.actransit.org)* serves Almeda and Contra Costa Counties.

The **Bay Area Traveler Information System** provides information for all transportation systems in the Bay Area *(415-817-1717; www.transitinfo.org)*.

Must Know: Practical Information

The **Bay Area Rapid Transit** (**BART**) commuter rail line links San Francisco with cities in the East Bay *(see map below; 415-989-2278; www.bart.gov)*. Fares are determined on a per-mileage basis. Trains operate Mon–Fri 4am–midnight, Sat 6am–midnight, Sun 8am–midnight.

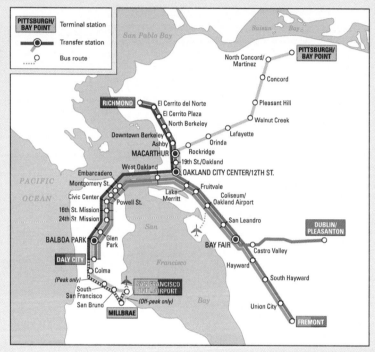

By Taxi – All San Francisco taxicab companies share the same rate schedule: $1.70 for the first mile and $1.80 for each additional mile. Taxis may not be readily available; it's best to call for a pickup. Major cab companies in the city include **Yellow Cab** *(415-626-2345)*, **Veterans** *(415-552-1300)* and **National** *(415-648-4444)*.

Cable Cars

What would a visit to San Francisco be without a ride on a cable car? Invented by Andrew Smith Hallidie in 1873, the city's signature public transportation system carries some ten million passengers each year. Today, 40 cable cars operate along three lines: Powell-Hyde, Powell-Mason and California Street *(daily 6am–12:30am)*. You can board a cable car about every five minutes at any stop (marked by brown signs) along the route. However, the cars tend to fill up as the day goes on, especially on weekends and in summer. Your best bet is to get on at the end of the line, the cable-car turnaround at Powell and Market streets. You can pay onboard *($3 one way)* or buy a book of tickets at the visitor information center located on Hallidie Plaza *(900 Market St.)*. CityPass booklets include passes for BART and the cable cars. Ticket booths are located at Powell and Market streets and at Hyde and Beach streets (two ends of the line). MUNI passports for one *($9)*, three *($15)*, or 7 *($20)* days are available at information booths at the airport or online at www.sfmuni.com. To learn more about this unusual transportation system, visit the Cable Car Museum *(1201 Mason St.; see Museums)*.

Must Know: Practical Information

FOREIGN VISITORS

Visitors from outside the US can obtain information from the San Francisco Convention and Visitors Bureau (415-391-2000; www.sfvisitor.org) or from the US embassy or consulate in their country of residence. For a complete list of American consulates and embassies abroad, visit the US State Department Bureau of Consular Affairs listing on the Internet at: http://travel.state.gov/links.html.

Entry Requirements – Travelers entering the United States under the Visa Waiver Program (VWP) must have a machine-readable passport. Any traveler without a machine-readable passport will be required to obtain a visa before entering the US. Citizens of VWP countries are permitted to enter the US for general business or tourist purposes for a maximum of 90 days without needing a visa. Requirements for the Visa Waiver Program can be found at the Department of State's Visa Services Web site (http://travel.state.gov/vwp.html).

All citizens of non-participating countries must have a visitor's visa. Upon entry, nonresident foreign visitors must present a valid passport and round-trip transportation ticket. Canadian citizens are not required to present a passport or visa, but they must present a valid photo ID and proof of citizenship. Naturalized Canadian citizens should carry their citizenship papers.

US Customs – All articles brought into the US must be declared at the time of entry. Prohibited items: plant material; firearms and ammunition (if not for sporting purposes); meat or poultry products. For information, contact the US Customs Service, 1300 Pennsylvania Ave. NW, Washington DC 20229 (202-354-1000; www.cbp.gov).

Money and Currency Exchange – Visitors can exchange currency at the **Thomas Cook Currency Services** (2301 Shattuck Ave., Berkeley; 510-849-8520), **Bank of America** (345 Montgomery St.; 650-615-4700) or **American Express Travel Service** (455 Market St.; 415-536-2600; travel.americanexpress.com). For cash transfers, **Western Union** (800-325-6000; www.westernunion.com) has agents throughout San Francisco. Banks, stores, restaurants and hotels accept travelers' checks with photoidentification. To report a lost or stolen credit card: **American Express** (800-528-4800); **Diners Club** (800-234-6377); **MasterCard** (800-307-7309); **Visa** (800-336-8472).

Driving in the US – Visitors bearing valid driver's licenses issued by their country of residence are not required to obtain an International Driver's License. Drivers must carry vehicle registration and/or rental contract, and proof of automobile insurance at all times. Gasoline is sold by the gallon (1 gal=3.8 liters). Vehicles in the US are driven on the right-hand side of the road.

Electricity – Voltage in the US is 120 volts AC, 60 Hz. Foreign-made appliances may need AC adapters (available at specialty travel and electronics stores) and North American flat-blade plugs.

Taxes and Tipping - Prices displayed in the US do not include the California sales tax of 8.5%, which is not reimbursable. It is customary to give a small gift of money—a tip—for services rendered, to waiters (15–20% of bill), porters ($1 per bag), chamber maids ($1 per day) and cab drivers (15% of fare).

Time Zone - San Francisco is in the Pacific Standard Time (PST) zone, eight hours behind Greenwich Mean Time, and three hours behind New York City.

Must Know: Practical Information

Measurement Equivalents

Degrees Fahrenheit	95°	86°	77°	68°	59°	50°	41°	32°	23°	14°
Degrees Celsius	35°	30°	25°	20°	15°	10°	5°	0°	-5°	-10°

1 inch = 2.5 centimeters   1 foot = 30.48 centimeters
1 mile = 1.6 kilometers   1 pound = 0.45 kilograms
1 quart = 0.9 liters   1 gallon = 3.78 liters

ACCOMMODATIONS

For a list of suggested accommodations, see Must Stays.

An area visitors' guide including lodging directory is available *(free)* from the San Francisco Convention and Visitors Bureau.

Hotel Reservation Services:

San Francisco Convention and Visitors Center – 888-782-9673

San Francisco Reservations – 800-677-1570

Central Reservation Service – 800-555-7555

Youth Hostels – *www.norcalhostels.org*. A no-frills, inexpensive alternative to hotels, hostels are a great choice for budget travelers. Prices average $25–$75 per night.

San Francisco City Center – 685 Ellis St. 415-474-5721.

San Francisco Downtown – 312 Mason St. 415-788-5604.

San Francisco-Fisherman's Wharf – Upper Fort Mason, Bldg. 240. 415-771-7277.

Major hotel and motel chains with locations in San Francisco include:

Property	Phone	Web site
Best Western	800-780-7234	www.bestwestern.com
Comfort, Clarion & Quality Inns	877-424-6423	www.choicehotels.com
Crowne Plaza	888-303-1746	www.crowneplaza.com
Days Inn	800-329-7466	www.daysinn.com
Hilton	800-774-1500	www.hilton.com
Holiday Inn	800-465-4329	www.holiday-inn.com
Howard Johnson	800-446-4656	www.hojo.com
Hyatt	800-233-1234	www.hyatt.com
ITT Sheraton	888-625-5144	www.sheraton.com
Marriott	888-236-2427	www.marriott.com
Omni	800-843-6664	www.omnihotels.com
Radisson	888-201-1718	www.radisson.com
Ramada	800-228-2828	www.ramada.com
Ritz-Carlton	800-241-3333	www.ritzcarlton.com
Westin	888-625-5144	www.westin.com

SPORTS

San Francisco is a great place to be a spectator where sports are concerned. The city's major professional sports teams include:

Sport/Team	Season	Venue	Phone	Web site
Baseball/San Francisco Giants (National League)	Apr–Oct	SBC Park	415-972-2000	www.sanfranciscogiants.mlb.com
Baseball/Oakland Athletics (American League)	Apr–Oct	Network Associates Coliseum	510-638-4900	www.oakland.athletics.mlb.com
Football/San Francisco 49ers (NFL)	Sept–Dec	3Com Park	415-656-4949	www.sf49ers.com
Football/Oakland Raiders (NFL)	Sept–Dec	Network Associates Coliseum	510-569-2121	www.raiders.com
Basketball/Golden State Warriors (NBA)	Nov–Apr	The Arena at Oakland	510-986-2200	www.nba.com/warriors

A Moving Experience: Earthquakes

Although the chances of your experiencing an earthquake while you're in California are extremely slim, Mother Nature is nonetheless unpredictable, and it's good to know what precautions to take—just in case. The last big tremblor to hit the Bay Area was the Loma Prieta quake of 1989. If an earthquake should hit while you're in town, here's what to do:

• If you're outside, move to an open area away from trees, buildings or power lines.

• If you're in a vehicle, pull over to the side of the road and stop. Don't park under bridges or sit on the floor of the car.

• If you're in a building, stand within a doorway or sit under a sturdy table. Stay away from windows and outside walls.

• Stay in a safe place until the shaking stops, and, if possible, stay tuned to the local radio or TV station for advisories.

San Francisco

Beauty By The Bay: San Francisco

Outsiders have been known to call San Franciscans smug. Why do so many of them walk around smiling? Is it the air? The food? The yoga studios? Ask any of them, and they'll be happy to tell you: they live in the best, most beautiful city in the world.

For more than two centuries, European explorers traveling by ship sailed right by the "Golden Gate," as the narrow, fog-cloaked entrance of San Francisco Bay came to be called. This entrance was discovered in 1769 by an overland scouting party from Mexico, which was then under Spanish rule. More Spaniards soon arrived, building a small fort called the Presidio and a Catholic missionary outpost, Mission Dolores *(see Historic Sites)*.

The Spanish mandate was to colonize the land and pacify the natives, but the soil was poor for agriculture and the natives proved reluctant converts. Thousands fled or died of European diseases; others retaliated and were killed. By the time Mexico won its independence from Spain in 1821 and gave the natives land of their own, it was too late. Demoralized, the tribes surrendered their shares to the powerful ranching families known as the Californios.

Noe. De Haro. Bernal. Vallejo. Many streets, neighborhoods and towns in the Bay Area were named after the rancheros, who prospered for about 25 years. Gradually a scrappy village—Yerba Buena (Spanish for "good herb")—took root on the tip of the San Francisco Peninsula. California became part of the United States in 1846, and in 1847 Yerba Buena's name was changed to San Francisco.

In 1848 gold was discovered at Sutter's Mill near Sacramento, and by 1849, some 90,000 hungry prospectors—called "forty-niners"—descended on the

> "What is this mysterious amalgam that keeps on working?. . . It is almost in the realm of the metaphysical: a brew of gold rushes and silver bonanzas, sailing ships and shrouded dawns, overnight fortunes and brilliant disasters, bootleg gin, champagne suppers, minestrone and Peking Duck, new-old, beautiful-ugly—a city like no other. . . . San Francisco lives!"
>
> Herb Caen, 1967

city. It was a rambunctious time. Brothels, flophouses, gambling halls, and opium dens were rife, as were, perhaps surprisingly, opera houses and theaters.

Natural disaster struck on the morning of April 18, 1906, in the form of a massive earthquake on the San Andreas Fault. By noon, 52 fires were burning throughout the city, eventually devouring 514 blocks and leaving 250,000 people homeless. Yet a plucky sprit prevailed in the refugee camps. The smoke had barely cleared when rebuilding began.

Over the next 50 years San Francisco took on its contemporary character. In the 1920s and 1930s, its progressivism came to the fore, as unions won major gains for workers, despite the Great Depression. Later the city opened its arms to mainstream society's outcasts—from the disaffected beat poets of the 1950s to idealistic flower children of the 1960s. Gay liberation and feminism, which took hold in the 1970s, are still powerful forces today.

Not that the city doesn't wear a suit once in a while. As computer companies flourished, city coffers bulged. In the late 1990s, hundreds of Internet start-ups set up shop in warehouses South of Market. The bubble burst in 2000, leaving nearly half of those offices vacant, but San Franciscans held their ground. In 2004 housing prices remained at an all-time high and the economy was rebounding.

Ups and downs are as much a part of the urban fabric as those outlandish hills. Like tourists thronging its cable cars, San Franciscans just hang on and enjoy the ride.

Fast Facts
• **Area:** 49 square miles
• **Population:** 790,000
• **Visitors:** 16 million annually
• **Number-one reason for visiting:** Atmosphere and ambience
• **Number of high rises (eight or more stories):** 501
• **Number of Victorian houses:** 14,000
• **Official Motto:** "Gold in peace, iron in war"

Landmarks

In most cities, landmarks are things that people build to add distinction. San Francisco, by contrast, had distinction before *anything* was built. Its undulating hills, expansive bay and dramatic fog all make it, in the words of Robert Redford, "the most beautiful place in the world." The following landmarks offer angles, both historical and cinematic, from which to appreciate it.

Alcatraz★★★

Access by ferry only (see sidebar below). 415-705-5555. www.nps.gov/alcatraz. Open daily May–Sept 9:30am–6:30pm. Rest of the year daily 9:30am–4:30pm. Closed Jan 1 & Dec 25. Ferry fee includes admission to island.

So close, and yet so far. Prisoners at "the Rock" had a tantalizing view of San Francisco, but the mile-and-a-half span between the two landmasses was for virtually unbridgeable. Would-be escapees drowned, froze or were eaten by sharks—if they weren't shot or captured first—and there was scant traffic in the other direction.

The first inmates came to Alcatraz in the 1850s, when a military fortress was established here by President Millard Fillmore. The military transferred jurisdiction

to the US Department of Justice in 1933. For the next 30 years, the penitentiary was home to the most "desperate and irredeemable criminals" in the US, including Al "Scarface" Capone, Machine Gun Kelly, and Robert "Birdman" Stroud. The conditions were unimaginably brutal, with one guard to every three prisoners, a strict no-talking policy, and "dark holes" of solitary confinement for rule breakers. Despite the odds of survival, 36 men tried to escape; it's still not clear if the most famous attempt, made by three men in 1962, was successful. Their bodies were never found.

Alcatraz was designated part of the Golden Gate National Recreation Area in 1972. Tours of the ruins have been fascinating visitors ever since. Don't miss the bleak concrete **cellhouse**★★, built by convicts in 1911.

Escape to Alcatraz

The Blue and Gold Fleet is the only line that offers service to Alcatraz. Ferries depart from Pier 41 on Fisherman's Wharf May–Sept daily 9:30am–4:15pm. Rest of the year until 2:15pm. 415-705-555. www.blueandgoldfleet.com. $20 adults.

The 15-minute ferry trip offers sensational **views**★★ of the city, the island, and the Golden Gate Bridge. Reservations for the ranger-led tours should be made at least a week in advance. Dress warmly and prepare to stay about two hours.

Coit Tower★★★

Summit of Telegraph Hill. 415-362-0808. www.coittower.org. Open May–Sept daily 10am–7:30pm. Rest of the year daily 10am–6pm. To avoid the steep climb, take the 39-Coit bus from Washington Square in North Beach.

Though less than a third of the height of the Trans-america Pyramid, this svelte 180ft column rivals that giant skyscraper as the city's best-known landmark. Why? In part because it's boosted into the clouds by 274ft **Telegraph Hill**★. But Coit Tower is also a monument to one resident's pride in her hometown.

As the story goes, when **Lillie Hitchcock Coit** (1843–1929) was a little girl in San Francisco, a firefighter rescued her from a burning building. Later, when she was 15, she came upon Knickerbocker Engine Company No. 5 struggling up Telegraph Hill en route to a blaze. Throwing down her schoolbooks, she rallied onlookers to help the firemen. To show their gratitude, they made her their mascot.

Coit remembered the incident for the rest of her life. In her will she left $125,000 to the city of San Francisco, the bulk of which went toward the con-struction of this tower, designed by Arthur Brown, Jr., and completed in 1934. (It was not meant to look like a firehose nozzle, as some locals persist in saying.)

Views★★★ – The top of the tower, reached via elevator and stairs, affords the best views in a city that, as Alfred Hitchcock said, doesn't have a bad angle. If you're afraid of heights, Pioneer Park at the base of the tower also has spec-tacular **views**★★★.

Murals★★ – In 1934, at the depth of the Great Depression, 26 out-of-work painters and their assistants were commissioned to create 19 fresco murals in the lobby of newly constructed Coit Tower. The theme, "contemporary life in California," was given a radical twist by the artists, who strongly identified with the thousands left penni-less, homeless, or unemployed by the stock market crash. Several of the painters clearly advocated revolution, which was a real possibility in a year that a general strike shut down the city for four days. Luckily, a movement to destroy the murals was voted down and the lobby was opened to the public in October 1934 to great acclaim.

Fisherman's Wharf★★★

Along Jefferson St. and the Embarcadero between Van Ness & Stockton Sts.
www.fishermanswharf.org.

Locals may avoid it like the plague, but this mile-long stretch of waterfront at the city's northern tip has blossomed over the past 50 years into San Francisco's most popular tourist attraction. Six piers jut out into the bay, offering everything from carousel rides and discount shopping (Pier 39) to maritime history (Hyde Street Pier). In between you'll find slips for the ferries to Alcatraz and Marin County.

This is not the city's original shoreline. Shortly after the Gold Rush, Henry "Honest Harry" Meiggs—councilman, entrepreneur, and later the most notorious embezzler of funds in the city's early history—constructed a wharf extending 1,600ft from present-day Francisco and Powell streets across North Point Cove into the bay. In the 1860s the cove (present-day North Beach) was filled with rock blasted from the eastern face of Telegraph Hill. A manufacturing and industrial zone grew up along this new flat stretch, which had clear access to the ships that at the time connected the burgeoning city with the rest of the world. Longshoremen and sailors ruled the roost.

And yes, there were fishermen. From the 1870s onward, most were of Italian descent, and their

influence lives on in the restaurants of the area. By the 1950s, the bay had been overfished, forcing fleets out into the ocean, and the shipping industry had moved to Oakland. Tourism, starting with the opening of the National Maritime Museum in 1951, saved the area from decline even as it obscured much of the history it meant to celebrate.

Tips for Visiting Fisherman's Wharf

As with most sites in the city, public transportation is the best way to get to Fisherman's Wharf. Take the Powell-Hyde cable car to its northern terminus if you want to visit the more historical western end of the wharf. The F-Market streetcar will deposit you at the east end, next to **Aquarium of the Bay★** . Jefferson Street is thronged on most weekends throughout the year; try a weekday if you want to avoid at least some of the crowds. For lunch, consider getting a ladle of creamy clam chowder in a hollowed-out loaf of sourdough bread, the wharf's signature dish.

Hyde Street Pier ★★

Jefferson St. at Hyde St. 415-561-7100. www.nps.gov/safr/local/top.html. Open year-round daily 9:30am–5pm. Closed Jan 1, Thanksgiving Day & Dec 25.

Once a ferry terminal, the westernmost pier of Fisherman's Wharf now showcases six historic ships, part of San Francisco Maritime National Historical Park. The grandest is the **Balclutha ★★**, a three-masted, square-rigger launched in Glasgow, Scotland, in 1886. The **Eureka ★**, a sidewheel ferry built in 1890, still ranks as the world's largest floating wooden structure. The **C.A. Thayer ★**, an 1895 codfisher, is one of only two three-masted wooden sailing schooners in the US *(C.A. Thayer is in dry dock for a major overhaul until late 2005)*.

The Cannery ★★ – *2801 Leavenworth St. See Must Shop.*

Ghirardelli Square ★★ – *900 North Point St. See Must Shop.*

USS Pampanito ★★ – *Pier 45. 415-775-1943. www.maritime.org. Open late May–early Oct daily 9am–8pm. Rest of the year daily 9am–6pm (Fri & Sat until 8pm).* A terrific self-guided audio tour of this World War II-era submarine captures the claustrophobia, fear and boredom of life underwater.

SS Jeremiah O'Brien ★ – *Pier 45. 415-544-0100. www.ssjeremiahobrien.org. Open year-round daily 9am–4pm. Closed Jan 1, Thanksgiving Day & Dec 25.* This lovingly restored 441ft vessel formed part of the 5,000-ship armada that stormed Normandy Beach in 1944. Self-guided tours explore the wheelhouse, crew's quarters and engine room (featured in the film *Titanic*).

National Maritime Museum ★ – *Beach St. at Polk St. See Museums.*

Pier 39 ★

Embarcadero at Stockton St. 415-705-5500. www.pier39.com. Open year-round Sun–Thu 11am–8pm, Fri & Sat 10am–8:30pm.

A theme-park atmosphere prevails on this double-decked shopping mall. If you can successfully dodge the crowds, you'll find 110 shops and restaurants, an **aquarium ★**, a large-format theater, a carousel, and more *(see Musts for Kids)*.

Playful Pinnipeds

One of San Francisco's modern mysteries is why, in January 1990, a boisterous pod of sea lions took up residence at Pier 39. Some say the 1989 Loma Prieta earthquake shook them out of their former digs; others credit the area's proximity to a large herring run. In any case, the original group of 50 told their friends and multiplied. Today up to 900 playful pinnipeds winter here, and some even stick around in the summer, when most of the pod shoves off for the Channel Islands.

Golden Gate Bridge★★★

Hwy. 101 between Marin County and San Francisco. 415-921-5858. www.goldengatebridge. org. Pedestrian access, via the east sidewalk, to the bridge daily 5am–9pm. $5 toll, southbound only.

Prepare to be amazed. The Golden Gate Bridge is truly astonishing. The balletic lines. The massive strength. The beautiful color. The staggering backdrop of sea and fog, craggy headlands and rocky shore and, in the distance, the little pastel outpost that is San Francisco ... It's no wonder the Golden Gate Bridge is one of the most photographed manmade structures on earth.

How did it come to be? The idea for a bridge over the narrow, treacherous strait where the San Francisco Bay meets the Pacific Ocean was first proposed in 1869 but dismissed over the ensuing four decades as unnecessary, structurally impossible and too expensive. By the early 20C, however, Marin County commuters started grumbling for an alternative to the ferry. In 1918 San Francisco's board of supervisors commissioned a feasibility study, but they balked at the proposed designs' price tags: some as high as $100 million. Enter Joseph Strauss, an experienced engineer who had already built more than 400 bridges around the world. When he said the job could be done for $27 million, people believed him, and public support for the project began to build.

Ground was broken in 1933, and for the next four years, thousands of men labored on the bridge, sinking its piers and anchorages into bedrock; erecting its two massive steel towers; draping three-foot-thick cables across the span; and building, piece by piece, the roadway to be suspended from those cables. Eleven men died during construction, but stringent safety procedures likely saved many others. The Golden Gate Bridge, which ended up costing $35 million, was inaugurated on May 27, 1937, to universal acclaim.

How the Golden Gate Bridge Measures Up

- **Height** – The roadway hangs 220ft over the water at high tide; the towers are 746ft (65 stories) tall.

- **Length** – The bridge measures 6,450ft (1.7mi) from end to end; the clear span between the towers is 4,200ft (1.22mi).

- **Strength** – The two main cables, which are anchored in place by 240-million-pound concrete blocks on either side of the bridge, measure 36 ⅜ inches in diameter and comprise 80,000mi of wire. The bridge contains a whopping 1.66 billion pounds of steel.

Lombard Street★★★

Between Hyde & Leavenworth Sts. See Musts for Fun.

In 1847, at a time when the city had one school and one newspaper and about 800 residents, Mayor Washington A. Bartlett hired Irish engineer Jasper O'Farrell to draw up a town plan. O'Farrell traced a rectangular grid over the peninsula, completely ignoring the city's extreme topography. Developers were left to fend for themselves if they wanted to build high into the hills. The cable car, invented in 1873, was the principal means of conquering hills without leveling them, but serpentine Lombard Street is pretty clever too. Its eight switchbacks, laid out in cobblestones in 1922, reduce the block's natural 27 percent grade to a workable 16 percent. Today roughly 750,000 drivers negotiate Lombard's hairpin turns each year, though it's also fun to walk alongside it or view it from the cable car that rattles along its summit.

Steepest Blocks of San Francisco
- Filbert between Hyde & Leavenworth (Russian Hill): 31.5% grade
- Jones between Union & Filbert (Russian Hill): 29% grade
- Duboce between Buena Vista & Alpine (Haight-Ashbury): 27.9% grade
- Lombard between Hyde & Leavenworth (Russian Hill): 27% grade
- Jones between Green & Union (Russian Hill): 26% grade
- Webster between Vallejo & Broadway (Pacific Heights): 26% grade
- Duboce between Alpine & Castro (Haight-Ashbury): 25% grade
- Jones between Pine & California (Nob Hill): 24.8% grade
- Fillmore between Vallejo & Broadway (Pacific Heights): 24% grade

Swensen's Ice Cream

Union Street at Hyde Street. 415-775-6818.

San Franciscans don't cope well with hot weather. So when native son Earle Swensen found himself on a troop ship in the South Pacific during World War II, he volunteered to make ice cream to cool the men down. Afterward he returned to his hometown and perfected his recipe at this, the flagship of Swensen's 400-strong fleet of ice-cream parlors.

Bay Bridge★★

I-80 between San Francisco and Oakland. $2 toll, westbound only.

Long considered the ugly little sister of the Golden Gate Bridge, the San Francisco-Oakland Bay Bridge (1936) is undergoing an extensive redesign to make it safer, more attractive, and, for the first time, accessible to bicycle traffic and pedestrians. Due to the tremendous distance it must span—8.5mi—the bridge has always consisted of two sections. The western section—two suspension bridges set end to end—that links San Francisco to Yerba Buena Island will remain untouched. In January 2002 work began on converting the east span, a chunky, cantilever-truss bridge between the island and Oakland, into an elegant, more flexible suspension bridge. The bridge's two levels will be replaced by a single, wider roadway, not only avoiding the "sandwiching" effect that happened when the top level collapsed in the 1989 Loma Prieta earthquake, killing 63 people, but allowing all drivers panoramic views of the San Francisco skyline and the East Bay hills.

City Hall★★

Civic Center, bounded by Grove, McAllister, Polk & Van Ness Sts. 415-554-4000. www.sfgov.org/site/cityhall_index.asp. Open year-round Mon–Fri 8am–8pm, Sat noon–4pm. Closed major holidays. Free docent-led tours held regularly; call 415-554-6023.

One of the only remnants of Daniel Burnham's plan to turn San Francisco into a "city beautiful," with grand Classical structures lording over spoked streets and prim, stately parks, City Hall (1915) is an impressive four-story building covering two city blocks. Its most distinguished feature is its regal dome, which is trimmed in gold-leaf and rises 13ft taller than that of the US Capitol in Washington, DC. The rows of Doric pillars and colonnades are typical of the Beaux-Arts style favored by its architect, Arthur Brown Jr. Within, a spiraling marble staircase ascends to a spectacular 181ft open rotunda.

"The lobby is officially known as the great central court, and it's like some Central American opera house: marble, arches, domes, acanthus leaves and Indian sandstone, quirks and galleries, and gilt filigrees, like Bourbon Louis curlicues of gold in every corner, along every molding, every flute, every cusp, every water-leaf and cartouche, a veritable angels' choir of gold, a veritable obsession with gold . . . and all kept polished as if for the commemoration of the Generalissimo's birthday."

Tom Wolfe,
Radical Chic & Mau-Mauing the Flak Catchers, 1970

Ferry Building★★

Embarcadero at Market St. 415-693-0996. www.ferrybuildingmarketplace.com. Open Mon–Fri 10am–6pm, Sat 9am–6pm, Sun 11am–5pm. Extended hours in summer.

The hugely successful Ferry Building renovation, completed in 2004, has brought this long-neglected landmark back into the spotlight as an airy retail and restaurant complex. Designed by A. Page Brown, the 1898 steel-reinforced sandstone structure is distinguished by its 244ft **clock tower**. During the peak years of ferry service, in the early 1930s, nearly 50,000 people passed through the vaulted nave each day. That number plummeted upon the opening of the bridges in 1936 and 1937, though, and slowly the building fell into disuse. The 1957 construction of the elevated Embarcadero Freeway effectively severed the Ferry Building from the Financial District for 35 years. Damaged by the 1989 earthquake, the highway was dismantled and the Ferry Building was returned to its former grandeur. It now shines as the city's premier showcase for local produce and gourmet goodies *(see Must Shop and Musts for Fun)*.

Taylor's Refresher

One Ferry Building. 866-328-3663. www.taylorsrefresher.com.
In early 2004, this popular roadside drive-in from Napa Valley opened a San Francisco outpost in the Ferry Building. Fans claim that Taylor's serves the best burgers in town, along with fish tacos, garlic fries and hand-scooped milkshakes. With access to all the farm produce at the Ferry Building Marketplace, Taylor's fast food is fresh indeed.

St. Francis Hotel★★

335 Powell St., Union Square. 415-397-7000. www.westin.com. See Must Stay.

San Francisco's second-oldest hotel was built overlooking Union Square by railroad baron Charles Crocker, who felt his city needed world-class accommodations. The hotel even survived the 1906 earthquake intact, but the ensuing fire gutted the interior. No matter. It was quickly rebuilt (and enlarged), opening in 1907. It has been a magnet for bigwigs ever since. Hemingway hunkered down here. So did Queen Elizabeth II, the Shah of Iran, and all US presidents since Taft. Step inside to ogle the entrance hall, with its coffered ceilings, travertine marble and ornate balconies. The Magneta grandfather clock has long been a favorite rendezvous point for city socialites

Compass Rose – Step up from the hotel's Powell Street lobby into this sumptuous bar and cafe, where afternoon high tea *(3pm–5pm)* is a St. Francis tradition. Pay high just for the pleasure of receiving your change—the hotel makes a point of washing its coins.

Palace of Fine Arts★★

Baker & Beach Sts. www.exploratorium.edu/palace.

Roman ruins in San Francisco? You might think so when you see the Palace of Fine Arts with its grand open rotunda. The rotunda is your clue to recognizing this well-known landmark, whether you're cruising the bay, visiting the Golden Gate Bridge, or shopping in the Marina district where the Palace is located.

Architect Bernard Maybeck designed the Palace to house art exhibits for the Panama-Pacific International Exposition of 1915 *(below)*. The building, distinguished by its 110ft-high-by-135ft-wide rotunda and surrounding colonnade, was only designed to last two years. Framed in wood, steel and chicken-wire, the Palace was covered with a plaster and burlap-fiber mixture called "staff." The structure's surface was then sprayed to look like travertine marble.

When the fair buildings were torn down to make way for residential development, aesthetically minded citizens lobbied to spare the Palace of Fine Arts. No efforts were made to shore up the building, however, and it slowly disintegrated until a plan to restore it was initiated in 1962. By making casts of each column and detail, and then razing the old sections, the building was entirely reconstructed from concrete and steel between 1964 and 1967. Today the rotunda, with its eight large relief panels illustrating Greek culture, is mirrored in the waters of the duck pond at its feet.

Exploratorium★★

3601 Lyon St., behind the Palace of Fine Arts rotunda.
See Musts for Kids.

The Panama-Pacific International Exposition of 1915

San Franciscans, rejuvenated by their city's resurrection from the 1906 earthquake and fire, and eagerly anticipating the completion of the Panama Canal, sought a way to celebrate that would also draw attention away from Los Angeles, their chief competitor in the shipping industry. Their answer was the Panama-Pacific International Exposition. With a collection of pavilions designed by some of the era's best architects, the exposition represented 25 countries and 29 states. An airplane could fly through the Great Palace of Machinery, and the Oregon state pavilion stood as a redwood Parthenon. More than 20 million people visited the fair in its 10 months of operation. Today, only the Marina Yacht Harbor and the Palace of Fine Arts stand as remnants of this grand affair.

Transamerica Pyramid★★

600 Montgomery St. between Washington & Clay Sts. www.tapyramid.com.

Though it lords over the Financial District in imperial fashion, San Francisco's tallest building is not, in fact, its tallest structure—that designation goes to Sutro Tower, a two-pronged television transmitter perched atop the city's highest peak. But the Transamerica Pyramid is without a doubt the more distinctive landmark.

Rising 48 stories to a crisp white point, it was designed by the Los Angeles firm of William Pereira and Associates in 1969 and completed in 1972. San Franciscans grumbled about the structure at first, feeling it ostentatious and too modern for their quaint little burg, but now it's roundly hailed as an architectural gem. The pyramid was specially designed to withstand earthquakes and tremors. Though built on landfill, not bedrock, it has a 52ft-deep steel and concrete foundation that moves with quakes, and a unique truss system to support the upper stories. At the 29th floor, two concrete wings rise vertically from the structure's tapering walls to accommodate elevator shafts that otherwise would have cut into the precious high-floor office space. A single private conference room on the 48th floor boasts 360-degree views of the city and the bay. A hollow lantern takes up the top 212ft of the pyramid.

Virtual Visit – Unfortunately, due to security concerns, the general public is not allowed inside the Transamerica Pyramid at this time. However, a street-level "virtual observation deck" has been set up on Washington Street. There you can look down at the city via rooftop cameras. Better yet, take a seat in adjacent Redwood Park, a pleasant, half-acre grove of some 40 redwood trees, and look up.

Jackson Square★★

Bounded by Washington, Montgomery & Sansome Sts., and Pacific Ave.
Venture north of the pyramid to one of San Francisco's oldest districts, a tiny enclave of two- and three-story brick buildings that miraculously survived the 1906 earthquake and fire; many date back to the 1850s. Pacific Avenue was for years the city's rowdiest street, crammed as it was with saloons, dance halls, gambling parlors, brothels and boarding houses for transient sailors. As you'll see, it has mellowed out quite a bit. At 463 Jackson, Challiss House sells some of the finest antiques in the US *(415-397-6999; www.challisshouse.com).*

Just as San Francisco has microclimates—patches of sun and fog—it also has what could be called microcultures. These are its neighborhoods. Each has its own character, a special quality that is generated, not surprisingly, by the people who live there. So spend some time strolling the city streets and be transported into these fascinating self-sustaining worlds.

Chinatown★★★

Roughly bounded by Bush, Stockton & Kearny Sts., and Columbus Ave. & Broadway. www.sanfranciscochinatown.com.

Teeming Chinatown spills down the eastern slope of Nob Hill, bridging the Financial District and North Beach. Within its 24 compact blocks you'll find a whole world. Streets and alleyways are lined with savory restaurants and dim sum "palaces," tea shops, vegetable markets, jewelry stores and temples.

The district got its start around 1849, when thousands of Cantonese treasure seekers crossed the Pacific and ventured up toward Sutter's Mill in search of gold. By the 1860s, Chinatown was well established. Bound by culture and language, residents also stuck together for safety. During the economic depressions of the 1870s, riotous bands of unemployed Anglos periodically stormed Chinatown, beating and sometimes killing men who, they felt, stole their jobs by working for lower wages. The Chinese Exclusion Act of 1882 effectively barred thousands of Chinese laborers (though not merchants) from bringing their families to the States. As a result, Chinatown was predominantly male well into the 20C. Opium dens, brothels and gambling halls proliferated, and turf wars regularly broke out among the "tongs," or local gangs, to control profits.

Conditions improved after the Exclusion Act was repealed in 1943 and more legitimate businesses took hold. Today the neighborhood, one of the most densely populated in the country with some 30,000 residents, remains a tight-knit community that fiercely protects its Asian heritage.

Chinese New Year Parade

Crowds fill the streets and the sound of thousands of popping firecrackers fills the night air each year *(date varies from late Jan–late Feb)* as the Chinese New Year Parade makes its raucous way through downtown. The largest celebration of its kind outside China, San Francisco's Chinatown event rings in the lunar new year with brightly costumed stilt walkers, acrobats, lion dancers and the grand finale—the 200ft-long Golden Dragon, decorated with colored lights and carried by a cadre of 100 people. *For information, check online at www.visitsf.org or www.sanfranciscochinatown.com.*

The Streets of Chinatown

Grant Avenue★★ – *See Must Shop.* Chinatown's Main Street, the eight blocks of Grant Avenue between Bush Street and Broadway abound in architectural chinoiserie: brightly painted balconies, curved tile rooflines, and staggered

towers. The ceramic carp and dragons on the roof of the **Chinatown Gate** *(Grant Ave. at Bush St.)* represent good luck.

Portsmouth Square★ – *Bounded by Clay, Kearny & Washington Sts.* Chinatown centers on Portsmouth Square, a small park where residents practice t'ai chi in the mornings and socialize into the night. It was here in 1846 that Captain John Montgomery officially claimed the city, then called Yerba Buena, for the US.

Stockton Street★ – Shoppers throng the produce, fresh fish and poultry markets flanking the four blocks between Clay Street and Broadway.

Waverly Place★ – *Off Washington St. between Grant Ave. & Stockton St.* This two-block alley is one of Chinatown's most colorful. Balconies are painted in symbolic hues: red for happiness, green for longevity, black for money, and yellow for luck.

Chinese Historical Society of America Museum – **[R]** *See map. 965 Clay St. 415-391-1188. www.chsa.org. Open year-round Tue–Fri 11am–4pm, weekends noon–4pm.* The society's exhibits explore the role of Chinese immigrants in the Western world in both the past and present.

Financial District★★

The Financial District is very much a place of business, and its character changes completely at different times of day. Traffic, pedestrians, and wildly pierced and tattooed bicycle messengers clog the streets during morning and evening rush hours *(7am–9am & 4pm–6pm)*. Take-out sandwich shops and salad bars do a brisk business at lunch. But at night the area is practically deserted—plan accordingly.

Despite its modern appearance, the Financial District harbors some of the city's earliest history. It was here, along what was then a sheltered cove, that the village of Yerba Buena grew up in the 1840s. At the outbreak of the Mexican-American War in 1846, US troops took control of the town from the Spanish-speaking *Cali-*

fornios and renamed it San Francisco. Until 1848 there were fewer than 500 residents. Then came the Gold Rush of 1849. Within months, some 90,000 treasure-hungry transients had converged on the settlement, some opening businesses to serve the exploding population. A city was born.

Half of what we think of as the Financial District didn't even exist then. Present-day Montgomery Street was a muddy path along the shoreline of the bay. But because nearly everyone at that time came by boat, there was a huge need for piers. Jutting out from the shore, the piers got longer and longer, essentially becoming roads. Soon the space between was filled with the remains of Rincon Hill, an inconvenient protuberance south of Market. Hundreds of abandoned ships were buried.

The 1906 earthquake and fire destroyed the district, but it was largely rebuilt by 1909. Many of the new buildings were done in the Classical style; then in the 1920s the first skyscrapers started going up. By the 1970s, after the Transamerica Pyramid was erected, preservationists were starting to panic and strict limitations were placed on the height and bulk of new buildings. Since then most new construction has happened South of Market *(see p 43)*.

Financial District Highlights

Bank of America Center★★ – *555 California St*. The city's largest building, this 52-story, dark-red behemoth (1971, Skidmore, Owings, and Merrill) competes with the Transamerica Pyramid for dominance of the skyline. A grand, panoramic **view** extends from the top-floor **Carnelian Room** lounge, which opens at 3pm *(one-drink minimum to enter; dress is business casual; 415-433-7500)*.

Tadich Grill

240 California St. 415-391-1849. Closed Sun.
Fresh fish is the fare, bulls and bears the topic of choice at this San Francisco institution, which began life as a coffee stand during the Gold Rush. Go for the charcoal-grilled sole, for the cold seafood salads, and for the no-nonsense service by white-jacketed waiters.

Bank of California★★ – *400 California St.* Now the Union Bank of California, this exquisite, classically proportioned bank (1907, Bliss and Faville) displays the energy and resources put into rebuilding the city after the 1906 fire. A regal, coffered ceiling tops the banking hall.

First Interstate Center★★ – *345 California St.* Two angular towers linked by a glass-enclosed "sky bridge" cap this futuristic skyscraper, designed in 1987 by the prestigious firm of Skidmore, Owings and Merrill.

Hallidie Building★★ – *130-150 Sutter St.* One of San Francisco's most note-worthy works of architecture, the seven-story office block was designed by Willis Polk, completed in 1917, and named after Andrew Hallidie, inventor of the cable car. Because the facade is formed by a modular grid of glass panes hanging from a reinforced concrete frame, the building is considered the world's first glass-curtain-walled structure.

Jackson Square★★ – *Bounded by Washington, Montgomery & Sansome Sts. and Pacific Ave. See Landmarks.*

Palace Hotel★★ – *2 New Montgomery St. 415-392-8600. www.luxuryresortcollection.com/palacehotel.* Constructed in 1875 by financier William Ralston, the Palace gained a reputation as the most opulent hotel in the West until it was gutted in the 1906 fire. The Palace reopened in 1909, and today the **Garden Court**★★, with its stunning leaded-glass canopy, is the hotel's most luxurious public space *(to see it, enter at 639 Market St.).*

Transamerica Pyramid★★ – *600 Montgomery St. See Landmarks.*

Union Square★★ – At the Financial District's western edge is Union Square, a formal park named on the eve of the Civil War, when it hosted numerous rallies in support of the Union. Spiffed up with a new granite plaza in 2002, the square now forms the centerpiece of a posh retail district *(see Must Shop).*

Belden Place

A piece of Old World Europe transplanted to San Francisco, this one-block-long alley extends from Pine to Bush Street just east of Kearny Street. It is lined with exquisite cafes serving international fare—French (Plouf and Cafe Bastille), Catalan (B44), and Creole (Erzulie), just to name a few.

Nob Hill★★

The upscale residential district lodged between Pacific Heights and China-town, Nob Hill got its name for the titans of industry who once lived here—"nob" is a contraction of "nabob," a term for European adventurers who made huge fortunes in India and the East.

These nabobs came in two waves. The first were the "Big Four" railroad mag-nates, Leland Stanford, Charles Crocker, Mark Hopkins and Collis Huntington. Formerly middle-class Sacramento merchants, these newly minted millionaires built sprawling mansions atop Nob Hill in the 1870s. In the 1880s they were joined by two of the four "Bonanza Kings," James Fair and James Flood, who profited mightily off Nevada's Comstock silver lode. Engineer Andrew Halli-die's "folly," the cable car, brought more development to the 376ft summit after the establishment of the California (1878) and Powell Street (1888) lines. The only structure to withstand the 1906 earthquake and fire was Flood's 1885 brownstone mansion, now the exclusive Pacific-Union Club *(1000 California St.)*. Today one of the best **views**★★★ in the city can be had from the **Top of the Mark** bar in the Mark Hopkins Hotel *(see Nightlife)*.

Cable Car Museum★★ – *121 Mason St. at Washington St. See Museums.*

Fairmont Hotel★★

Main entrance on Mason St. between California & Sacramento Sts. 415-772-5000. www.fairmont.com. See Must Stay.

In one of her first big commissions, architect Julia Morgan oversaw the restoration of this Italian Renaissance hotel, which was nearly complete when the 1906 earthquake struck. On April 18, 1907, exactly one year later, the Fairmont re-opened. The ornate main lobby, with its massive marble pillars and wrought-iron balconies, is

worth a peek, as is the supremely kitschy Tonga Room *(see Nightlife)*.

Grace Cathedral★

1051 Taylor St. at California St. 415-749-6300. www.gracecathedral.org.

The third-largest Episcopal cathedral in the US, completed in 1964, anchors the crest of Nob Hill, its French Gothic spires soaring majestically over the city. The bronze **Gates of Paradise**★ in the eastern portal are the cathedral's most prized architectural feature; at 16ft high, they are divided into 10 richly ornamented panels depicting scenes from the Old Testament.

Hobnob Tours

To get a thorough grounding in Nob Hill history, take the HobNob walking tour, which departs weekdays from the Fairmont Hotel *(2 ½ hrs; 10am & 1:30pm; 866-851-1123; www.hobnobtours.com)*.

North Beach★★

One of the sunniest and liveliest neighborhoods in the city gets its character from the Italians who came to dominate the area around 1900. Though they're no longer in the majority residentially, the dozens of cafes, restaurants, delicatessens and bars here attest to their interpretation of "the good life." A ragtag assortment of beret-wearing poets and artists who called themselves the "beat generation" shared this view from the mid-1950s to the mid-1960s. They were driven out by the busloads of tourists who came through to see what all the fuss was about. Many Italian shopkeepers remained.

Columbus Avenue, the neighborhood's main thoroughfare, cuts diagonally from the Transamerica Pyramid to the Cannery on Fisherman's Wharf *(see Landmarks)*. It's packed with places to eat, drink and be entertained *(see Must Eat and Nightlife)*.

Coit Tower★★★ — *Atop Telegraph Hill. See Landmarks.*

Filbert Steps★★

If you're visiting Coit Tower on foot, be sure to take this steep, celebrated pathway down the east flank of Telegraph Hill. Views look out onto treehouse-like cottages and their well-tended gardens. The Streamline Moderne apartment house at 1360 Montgomery appeared in the 1947 Bogart-Bacall film *Dark Passage*.

City Lights Bookstore★ — *261 Columbus Ave. See Must Shop.* Beatnik Lawrence Ferlinghetti's book nook.

Saints Peter and Paul Church★
666 Filbert St. 415-421-0809.

Overlooking **Washington Square★**, North Beach's premier picnic park, the twin-spired church is fondly known as the Italian cathedral. Baseball great Joe DiMaggio, who grew up in the neighborhood, and screen legend Marilyn Monroe had wedding pictures taken in front of the church—but contrary to local lore, the two weren't married here. Step inside to see the spectacular 40ft-high altar, featuring a sculptural reproduction of Da Vinci's *Last Supper*.

Caffeine and Conversation

Besides making perfect cappuccinos, these bustling cafes offer a glimpse into the daily life of North Beach. Most are open from morning until midnight (or at least 10:30pm) and serve, in addition to coffee, wine and beer, pastries (cannoli!) and sandwiches.

Caffè Trieste – *601 Vallejo St. 415-392-6739.*
Mario's Bohemian Cigar Store – *566 Columbus Ave. 415-362-0536.*
Caffè Puccini – *411 Columbus Ave. 415-989-7033.*
Caffè Greco – *423 Columbus Ave. 415-397-6261.*
Tosca – *242 Columbus Ave. 415-986-9651. Open daily 5pm–2am.* A great place for a late-night cocktail, this 1940s-style bar plays only opera on its juke box.

Pacific Heights★★

Great for an afternoon stroll, this tony residential neighborhood holds some of the city's finest (and biggest) houses and loveliest views. The district stretches across a high, east-west ridge between Van Ness Avenue and the Presidio. After the 1906 quake and fire, many wealthy San Franciscans who had lost homes on Nob Hill resettled in Pacific Heights, where the parcels were bigger. Most of the district's mansions date from this period. Yet thanks to the neighborhood's distance from the downtown inferno, many "gingerbread" Victorians remain from the 1880s and 1890s. These were built for well-to-do families but were actually the "prefab" houses of the era: fish-scale shingles, ogive-shaped windows, and finely carved verge boards could be bought directly from lumber mills and added to the design.

When you visit, bear in mind that streets ascend and descend abruptly, sometimes as much as 100ft in one block. For an in-depth look at the neighborhood, consider taking the two-hour Pacific Heights Walking Tour offered by San Francisco Architectural Heritage *(Sun 12:30pm; for details, call Haas-Lilienthal House)*.

Haas-Lilienthal House★★

2007 Franklin St. 415-441-3004. www.sfheritage.org. Visit by guided tour only, Wed & Sat noon–3pm, Sun 11am–4pm. Closed major holidays. $8.

San Francisco's only fully furnished Queen Anne Victorian open to the public, this imposing gray edifice was built in 1886 for William Haas, a prominent wholesaler. It has patterned siding, ornately bracketed gables, and a deceptive corner tower with windows 10ft above the floor. Within, two parlors, a dining room, and one of the original six bedrooms reflect the period from the 1880s to the 1920s in their decor.

Spreckels Mansion★★

2080 Washington St. Not open to the public.

Of all the many grand mansions in Pacific Heights, none is more ostentatious than the French Baroque-style palace built in 1913 for sugar magnate Adolph Spreckels and his wife. Best-selling author Danielle Steel now lives here.

Shopping in Pacific Heights

Fillmore Street between Bush and Jackson streets is Pacific Heights' retail corridor. It's surprisingly unpretentious, with a browser-friendly blend of book shops and boutiques, as well as numerous cafes. For a good strong jolt of coffee, try **Peet's** *(2197 Fillmore St.; 415-563-9930)*. Nearby Cow Hollow also has some interesting shopping, along Union Street. *See Must Shop.*

Civic Center★

Bounded by Market St., Van Ness Ave. & Golden Gate Ave.

San Francisco's "town center," as it were, has one life during the day, when government offices are in full swing, and another at night, when concert goers flock to performances in its theaters. The Beaux-Arts buildings here are considered to be one of the finest groups of this style in the US.

Well into the 19C, city government occupied a variety of buildings girdling Portsmouth Square in present-day Chinatown. But in 1872 it was decided that something grander was in order. Finally, in 1905, architects Daniel Burnham of Chicago and Willis Polk, a local, presented what was called "the Burnham Plan," featuring grand monuments, wide boulevards, and other City Beautiful hallmarks to remake San Francisco along the lines of Paris or Washington, DC. After the 1906 catastrophe, however, most people simply rebuilt on the old street grid. Civic Center, a small-scale version of the plan, comes courtesy of the government that commissioned it.

In 1945 the area played a significant role in world history. From April to June, 1945, the United Nations convened in the War Memorial Opera House, and the UN Charter was signed in the Herbst Theatre.

Asian Art Museum★★★ – *200 Larkin St. See Museums.*

City Hall★★ – *Entrance on Polk St., between McAllister & Grove Sts. See Landmarks.*

San Francisco War Memorial and Performing Arts Center ★★

401 Van Ness Ave. 415-552-8338. Visit by guided tour only, Mon 10am–2pm (except holidays); $5. See Performing Arts.

Three exceptional buildings contain the city's most renowned performing-arts institutions, two of which saw the founding of the UN in 1945. On the north end is the **Veterans Building [F]** *(see map on inside front cover)* home to the (relatively intimate) 928-seat Herbst Theatre. The UN Charter was signed here. South of the Veterans Building is an attractive formal courtyard designed by Thomas Church.

The complex's centerpiece, the 1932 **War Memorial Opera House [E]** *(see map on inside front cover)*, was the first city-owned opera house in the US. The San Francisco Opera and Ballet perform in its 3,176-seat auditorium, which is distinguished by a 27ft star chandelier and a gold brocatelle proscenium curtain that weighs one ton. From April to June 1945, the Conference on International Organization met here to establish the UN's bylaws.

To the south stands the strikingly modern **Louise M. Davies Symphony Hall** (1980). Though some critics found its curving glass facade out of sync with the Beaux-Arts aesthetic of the area, it has proved a festive place to see a concert, and particularly appropriate to the challenging new repertoire championed by conductor Michael Tilson Thomas *(see Performing Arts)*.

San Francisco Public Library ★

100 Larkin St. 415-557-4400. http://sfpl.lib.ca.us.

Opened in 1996, the city's new library turns a contemporary eye on Beaux-Arts classicism. The gleaming exterior is sheathed in granite from the same quarry that provided stone for the City Hall and War Memorial. The seven-story interior is decked out with catwalk bridges, artworks, computers, and an asymmetrical skylit atrium. Changing displays of art and literature are presented in the lower-level Jewett Exhibition Gallery.

Hayes Valley

Just west of Civic Center, edgy Hayes Valley is a good place to dine or shop when you're in the area *(see Must Shop and Nightlife)*.

Dashiell Hammett Tour

Tours leave at noon from the northwest corner of the Main Library at 100 Larkin St. May–June and by appointment. 510-287-9540. www.donherron.com.
Foggy nights, deserted street corners, a fedora dipped below one eye, a trench coat with the collar up. Ever since John Huston shot *The Maltese Falcon* here, the city has become synonymous with mystery and intrigue. See the seedy bars and tawdry hotels so beloved by novelist Dashiell Hammett, who worked in San Francisco as a Pinkerton detective before creating his alter ego, Sam Spade. Don Herron knows his stuff: he's been leading these celebrated walks for 25 years.

Haight-Ashbury ★

Centered on Haight St. between Central Ave. & Stanyan St.

Although more than three decades have passed since the Human Be-In and the Summer of Love, a countercultural ethos still clings to the Haight, particularly on Haight Street itself. The stretch between Central and Stanyan streets, known to locals as the "Upper Haight," is packed with thrift stores, boutiques, and coffeehouses *(see Must Shop)*.

Ambitious fixer-uppers have made their homes here too, drawn by the tremendous concentration of Victorian homes—90 percent of the housing stock predates 1922. Stroll along Page, Masonic and Waller streets to see lovely examples of the fanciful Queen Anne style.

Mission District ★

Roughly bounded by 14th, Cesar Chavez, Dolores & Potrero Sts.

This sunny southern neighborhood has a young, funky feel, with artists, dot-commers, and activists coexisting with a vibrant Latino community. The Catholic Mission anchored a small village here in the early 1800s, but none of it remains. Instead you'll find shoulder-to-shoulder Italianate row houses, some dating to the 1870s.

Mission Dolores ★ – *16th & Dolores Sts. See Historic Sites.*

Maestrapiece

Women's Building, 3543 18th St. at Lapidge St.

Covering two exterior walls, this is one of the Mission's newest, biggest and most colorful murals, a celebration of the area's rich Latino and feminist heritage. Look for Georgia O'Keeffe, Audre Lorde and Rigoberta Menchu in the design.

Valencia Street – *See Must Shop.*

Anchor Brewing Company

1705 Mariposa St. (at De Haro St.). 415-863-8350. www.anchorbrewing.com. Free tour offered weekdays at 1pm. Reservations required; book 3-6 weeks in advance.
Here's where the whole microbrew movement started. Founded in 1896, Anchor began as one of many local breweries, but Prohibition and the decline of manufacturing that followed threatened to close its doors. Appliance heir Fritz Maytag bought the company in 1965 and perfected its tar amber ale after visiting breweries throughout Europe. Beer drinkers used to thin, flavorless lagers took to the stronger taste, and entrepreneurs nationwide copied Maytag's model. The extremely popular two-hour tour explains all aspects of production and ends with samples of each Anchor brew made (six and counting).

Russian Hill★

Bounded by Francisco, Taylor, Pacific & Polk Sts.

Along with neighbors Nob Hill and Telegraph Hill, Russian Hill offers some of the best vistas in the city, along with a glimpse of its largely forgotten literary history. As the story goes, the hill was named in the mid-19C when the graves of Russian seal hunters were discovered atop the crest of present-day Vallejo Street. But it wasn't until the 1880s, when the cable car provided easy access to its summit, that people actually started moving here en masse. The Powell-Hyde and Powell-Mason lines are still the best means to get to the top.

Literary Legacy – From 1856 through the 1890s, Catherine Atkinson's home at 1032 Broadway served as a salon for Mark Twain, Ambrose Bierce, Robert Louis Stevenson, and other big-name writers. Ina Coolbrith convened a similar group at her house at 1604 Taylor Street. Beat writer Jack Kerouac spent six months on the hill in 1952; he stayed with friends at 29 Russell Street and worked on several novels, including *On the Road*. Evidently the hill is an inspiring place.

Lombard Street★★★ – *See Landmarks.*

Views★★

The Taylor Street summit of the Vallejo Street Stairway—the centerpiece of Ina Coolbrith Park—offers magnificent eastward-facing views of the bay. At the corner of Jones and Green streets, views extend north over Alcatraz.

San Francisco Art Institute★

800 Chestnut St. See Museums.

Zazie

941 Cole St. 415-564-5332.
This tiny Provençal bistro, named after Louis Malle's film of the same name, is a local favorite for breakfast, lunch and dinner. Enjoy Belgian waffles with caramelized pecans, salade Niçoise, and an assortment of savory stews and sandwiches.

Castro District

Bounded roughly by 16th to 22nd Sts. and Douglass to Dolores Sts.
Epicenter of gay San Francisco, "the Castro," as it's called, hums with energy night and day. In the 1950s, enterprising gay designers began purchasing the Castro's 19C Victorians at rock-bottom prices and fixing them up. Though prices are significantly higher, the trend continues today.
The action's at **Castro Street** *(between Market & 20th Sts.)*, a thrumming corridor of shops and bars, and home to the **Castro Theatre**★ movie palace *(see Nightlife)*. **Market Street** *(between Castro & Church Sts.)* and **Church Street** *(between Market & 17th Sts.)* offer a fun mix of shops and restaurants that appeal to folks of all persuasions.

South of Market★

Roughly bounded by 12th, Market & King Sts. and the Embarcadero.

San Francisco's hard-scrabble history meets its high-tech future in the large, heterogeneous region known as South of Market, or SoMa. In 1847 city planner Jasper O'Farrell gave SoMa its distinctive look, making its streets twice as wide and its blocks four times as large as those north of market, and setting the whole area at a 45-degree angle to the grid. The idea was to make room for industry, and it worked. Foundries, gasworks, shipyards, refineries and breweries took hold here. As manufacturing declined in the mid-20C, architects, graphic designers, software companies, and publishers divvied up former industrial buildings and warehouses into loftlike offices. Other large spaces have been converted to restaurants, clubs and galleries *(see Nightlife)* or retail stores *(see Must Shop)* in this up-and-coming area.

San Francisco Museum of Modern Art★★ – *151 Third St. See Museums.*

SBC Park★★ – *Third & Kings Sts., at the Embarcadero. See Musts for Fun.*

Yerba Buena Gardens★★

Mission St. between Third & Fourth Sts. www.yerbabuena.org.

The funky younger sister of Civic Center, this family-friendly complex of parks and museums, galleries and theaters has quickly established itself as one of the city's most vital enter-tainment hubs. It centers on the rolling green **Esplanade**, a lawn used for picnics and outdoor concerts. A waterfall monument to Dr. Martin Luther King, Jr. provides an appro-priate backdrop.

Post-Modern **Yerba Buena Center for the Arts★ [K]** *(see map on inside front cover; Third & Mission Sts.; 415-978-2787; www.yerbabuenaarts.org)* hosts thoughtpro-voking art exhibits that change regularly. The building also contains a 750-seat theater *(see Performing Arts)*.

Metreon★, Rooftop at Yerba Buena Gardens★★ and **Zeum★** – *At Yerba Buena Gardens. See Musts for Kids.*

> ### Town Hall
> *342 Howard St. 415-908-3900. www.townhallsf.com.* Hearty regional American fare rules the roost at this new restaurant, three blocks east of Yerba Buena Gardens. Occupying a beau-tifully renovated 1907 ware-house, Town Hall suggests an Adirondack eating hall with its exposed brick walls and white wainscoting. If you want to make a new friend, grab a seat at the 14ft-long communal table by the bar and order the irresistible butterscotch and chocolate pot de crème.

Maybe you didn't come to the City by the Bay to visit museums. Sure, there's a ton of other things to do, but you'd be remiss if you didn't at least sample the city's cultural offerings. There's much for art lovers here, from the acclaimed Asian Art Museum to SF MOMA. And the Cable Car Museum and the Exploratorium are musts for the younger set.

Asian Art Museum★★★

200 Larkin St., Civic Center. 415-581-3500. www.asianart.org. Open year-round Tue–Sun 10am–5pm (Thu until 9pm). Closed Mon & major holidays. $10. Free admission the first Tue of every month.

Don't miss this star among San Francisco's diverse museums. The group of some 15,000 works owned by the Asian Art Museum spans 6,000 years and constitutes the largest museum in the US devoted to Asian art. Objects run the gamut from Chinese jades to Japanese kimonos and Islamic manuscripts to Korean celadons.

The museum was born in 1959, when Chicago millionaire Avery Brundage offered San Francisco a part of his vast collection of Asian art on the condition that the city build a museum to display it. Completed in 1966, the Asian Art Museum was located for 35 years in Golden Gate Park. Having long outgrown its original home, the museum opened in its spectacular new digs in the renovated 1917 Beaux-Arts-style San Francisco Public Library in March 2003. The expansive 29,000sq ft of gallery space is twice as big as the original museum, allowing for the display of some 2,500 artworks from the permanent collection.

Home Is Where The Art Is

The remarkable setting for this stellar collection was designed by Italian architect Gae Aulenti, whose credits include the Musée d'Orsay in Paris. She transformed the gloomy former library into a dramatic display space centering on an open sky-lit court. In the process, Aulenti preserved the historic building's prominent elements, such as the original marble staircase, columned loggia and great hall. One-third of $160 million spent on the renovation of the library building went to retrofit the structure in case of an earthquake. To protect its priceless collection, the whole museum now floats on an underground moat. If an earthquake were to shake the city, the building would move as one unit, gently balanced in the water.

A glass-enclosed escalator now whisks visitors up to the third floor where they work their way down through the 33 galleries on two floors that display objects from the permanent collection. Presented as the story of Asian culture, the collection is organized geographically (each region claims a different-colored gallery) and thematically—according to the spread of Buddhism, trade and interchange, and local beliefs and customs. In each room, artworks are displayed chronologically, from the oldest to the most recent. Eye-catching objects are placed in the middle of the galleries as visual lures to lead you into the next room. Back on the ground

floor, you'll find changing exhibits, an upscale museum shop, and **Café Asia**, featuring such pan-Asian fare as Bento boxes, sushi, noodle dishes, hot pots and rice bowls.

Highlights of the Collection

Free multilingual audio tours are available to introduce you to the museum's highlights. Here's a small taste to whet your appetite:

338 Buddha★★★ – The museum's prize, this small bronze statue is the oldest dated Chinese Buddha in existence; 338 refers to the year it was made.

Rhino ritual vessel★★ – This Shang Dynasty bronze vessel is unique for its animal shape.

Elephant throne★★ – The stunning silver throne was made in India c.1870–1920.

Indonesian rod puppets★★ – The museum's vivid set of 71 rod puppets is a rare find.

An authentic **Japanese tea room**★ on the second floor hosts tea ceremonies once a month *(be sure to make reservations well in advance as attendance is limited)*.

AsiaAlive

Drop by the museum's Grand Hall, the sumptuous former catalog room of the library, which is set off by a barrel-vaulted and coffered travertine marble ceiling, for interactive programs that focus on the diverse arts of Asia. Here's your chance to learn Afghan knotted-pile rug weaving or traditional Chinese painting techniques from experts in the arts—the theme changes each month. This is fun for the whole family, where you can meet the artists and watch them demonstrate their craft, then try your own hand at designing a miniature rug or creating a Chinese brush painting. Best of all, it's free. *Programs are offered daily in the second-floor Samsung Hall from 12pm–4pm (extended hours on Thu evenings)*.

Cable Car Museum★★

1201 Mason St. at Washington St. 415-474-1887. www.cablecarmuseum.com. Open daily Apr–Sept 10am–6pm. Rest of the year daily 10am–5pm. Closed Jan 1, Thanksgiving Day & Dec 25.

San Francisco's cable-car system is the only one of its kind in the world, and this is the place to see it in action. Besides being a museum, the weathered brick building on the steep north slope of Nob Hill does double duty as the cable-car barn and powerhouse for the city's fabled cable cars.

Head to the upper level, where you can stand on the balcony and gape at the thrumming cable-car mechanism. Each of the three cable lines in existence today has its own machinery here: a 510-horsepower DC electric motor, gears to control the speed of the motor, and a set of three huge pulleys, called sheaves. To keep the cable from slipping, each cable wraps around a set of powered sheave wheels and over and under unpowered wheels in a figure-8 pattern.

Downstairs, you'll find historic photographs and displays explaining how the cable cars came to be, as well as **Car No. 8**, the only surviving vehicle from the city's first cable-car line (1873). You can even ring a real cable-car bell—the sound that's synonymous with San Francisco. And don't leave the city without riding on a cable car *(see Musts for Fun)*.

Getting A Grip

Today's cable-car system uses the mechanism developed in 1873 by Scottish immigrant Andrew Hallidie, who came to California in 1852 to build a wire-rope transport system for the gold mines. Just as a constantly moving tow rope pulls a skier up a snowy slope, huge loops of steel cable run a continuous 9.5mph beneath Powell, Hyde, Mason and California streets. The cable is powered by electric motors at the Cable Car Barn *(above)*. To start the car moving, the "gripman" stands in the middle of the car and "throws" a lever that extends down through a slot in the street. At the underground end of the lever, a "grip" closes and opens like a jaw on the moving cable. The tighter the grip closes, the faster the car goes. To reduce speed, the gripman opens the grip to release the cable; he applies brakes to stop. A conductor at the rear of the car helps with braking when necessary.

California Academy of Sciences★★

Temporarily located downtown at 875 Howard St. The Golden Gate Park facility is closed to the public until its new building is completed in summer 2008. 415-750-7145. www.calacademy.org. Open year-round daily 10am–5pm. $7.

The oldest scientific institution in the West was founded in 1853 in a rush of post-Gold Rush enthusiasm to study California's natural resources. Over the years, the Academy evolved into three divisions: the **Natural History Museum**, with more than 14 million specimens; the **Steinhart Aquarium**, the oldest aquarium in the US; and the **Morrison Planetarium**.

The Academy's New Home

Over the years it has been in existence, the California Academy of Sciences managed to sprawl out into a complex of 12 buildings in Golden Gate Park. The design for the new Academy, conceived by Italian architect Renzo Piano (whose credits include the Centre Georges Pompidou in Paris), will unify the institution under one landscaped "living roof." Tucking the park around it, the new building will provide more square footage on a smaller footprint.

At present, the Academy is beginning a $370-million project to combine its separate exhibition spaces into one dynamic new facility that illustrates how all living things are interconnected. While the Academy's new building is being completed, you can see selected exhibits from the Steinhart Aquarium and the Natural History Museum at the Howard Street location. In order to set up its temporary digs downtown while the future facility is being built, the Academy will need to move some 18 million scientific specimens, including 844,891 flies, 2,761,004 beetles and more than 60,000 spiders and scorpions. Not to mention a 1,350-pound quartz cluster, more than a quarter of a million reptiles and amphibians, and thousands of fish.

Here's how the new facilities will shape up in 2008:

Natural History Museum★★ – One new exhibit will take visitors on a multi-level journey from the forest floor to the upper canopy of the rain forest, earth's most diverse habitat.

Morrison Planetarium★ – *Closed until 2008.* When it reopens, the planetarium will again provide glimpses into the heavens through state-of-the-art technology. Exhibits will reveal old and new discoveries about the cosmos.

Steinhart Aquarium★ – *Temporary location at 875 Howard St. See Musts for Kids.* The revamped aquarium will stress the essential role that aquatic environments play in our world with a new 225,000-gallon living coral reef.

California Palace of the Legion of Honor★★

100 34th Ave. at Clement St., in Lincoln Park. 415-863-3330. www.thinker.org. Open year-round Tue–Sun 9:30am–5pm. Closed major holidays. $8; free Tue.

Overlooking the Pacific Ocean from its remote perch aptly called Land's End, the Legion of Honor displays 4,000 years of ancient and European art. And what more fitting place to see splendid artwork than in architect George Applegarth's three-quarter-scale concrete version of the 18C Palais de la Légion d'Honneur in Paris? Founded by Alma and Adolph Spreckels, the Legion was dedicated on Armistice Day 1924 in honor of the 3,600 Californians who perished in World War I.

In 1995 the Legion underwent a three-year overhaul and seismic retrofitting that added an underground level and six new special-exhibition galleries surrounding a skylit court. Today its collection of some 83,750 objects includes European masterworks from the 14C to the 20C, European decorative arts, and antiquities from the ancient Mediterranean world and the Near East.

Art Patron With Attitude

Born in San Francisco to impoverished European immigrants, **Alma de Bretteville** (1881–1968) inherited the energy of her hard-working mother and the pride of her father, a descendant of the faded nobility of the French de Bretteville lineage, who instilled in his daughter a sense of noblesse oblige. Alma grew into a statuesque, willful, mostly self-educated woman who defied convention in many ways. After several years of a socially unacknowledged liaison, she married sugar magnate Adolph Spreckels in 1908.

In 1914 she met and fell under the influence of American-born dancer Löie Fuller, the toast of Belle Epoque Paris, who convinced Alma that her destiny was to become a great patron of the arts with Löie as her chief advisor. Alma took Löie's challenge to heart and in 1915, she convinced her husband to build a new art museum in San Francisco.

● In 1950 the Legion received the city-owned **Achenbach Foundation for Graphic Arts**, which includes more than 70,000 prints, drawings, and illustrated books spanning six centuries.

● The Legion of Honor owns 111 **Rodin** sculptures, which founder Alma Spreckels—who knew the sculptor personally—collected during Rodin's lifetime. You can see an original cast of Rodin's *Thinker* in the Court of Honor.

M.H. de Young Memorial Museum★★

On the Music Concourse in Golden Gate Park. 415-863-3330. www.deyoungmuseum.org. Closed until 2005 during construction of the museum's new building.

Badly damaged in the 1989 Loma Prieta earth- quake, the original de Young Museum has been demolished to make way for a new building. When it reopens, the de Young is where you'll find the West's foremost collection of art of the Americas, Oceania and Africa.

The de Young owes its existence to its name- sake, Michael H. de Young, co-founder of the *San Francisco Chronicle,* who founded the museum in 1895. Collecting with more enthusiasm than knowledge, de Young amassed a hodgepodge of artwork, historic artifacts and natural-history ex- hibits that was described at one point as consisting of "23,000 stuffed birds and eggs of every biped that ever had wings." Eventually, though, de Young attracted the attention of benefactors such as John D. Rockefeller, whose gift of American paintings and works on paper in 1978 propelled the museum to first-class status.

Thinking along the lines of "build it and they will come," the de Young is counting on its new facility to provide a West Coast showcase for prominent national collections as well as its own. When the new museum opens, it will emphasize American contributions to art by contrasting early-20C American art with late-20C works by artists in the Bay area.

What's in the Collection?

American Art★★ – The museum owns more than 1,000 paintings by American artists, from colonial times to the 20C.

Art of the Americas★ – Ancient objects from Mesoamerica, Central and South America make up the heart of this collection, which includes a 10ft totem pole from Alaska.

African Art – This rapidly growing collection highlights a cross-section of sub- Saharan cultures and illustrates some of the oldest traditions in art.

Oceanic Art – Works from Polynesia, Melanesia and Micronesia formed one of the charter collections of the museum.

The New de Young

Slated to open in 2005, the de Young's new contemporary structure of recycled redwood, eucalyptus and copper will fold culture into nature in Golden Gate Park. Herzon & de Meuron (whose credits include the new Tate Gallery of Modern Art in London) are the architects; according to their design, the new museum will occupy two fewer acres than the original, yet have double the gallery space. A ten-story Education Tower with an observation deck will rise at the museum's northeast corner. Outside, plantings of native flora—palm trees, redwood, cypress, ferns—will serve to further link the structure to the park around it.

Museums

San Francisco Museum of Modern Art★★

[M⁹] *refers to map on front inside cover. 151 3rd St. 415-357-4000. www.sfmoma.org. Open Memorial Day–Labor Day Thu–Tue 10am–5:45pm. Rest of the year Thu–Tue 11am–5:45pm (Thu until 9pm). Closed Wed & major holidays. $10.*

SF MOMA, as it's known, stands out for its eye-catching architecture as much as for its collection. You can pick the museum out from the South of Market skyline by its signature 125ft-tall cylindrical tower. Swiss architect Mario Botta slanted the top of the cylinder toward Third Street and faced the angled surface with glass in order to create a huge skylight that floods the upper galleries with natural light. Rows of black and white granite on the shaft contrast with the red brick of Botta's post-Modern museum building.

Founded in 1935, San Francisco's premier showcase for modern art moved into its new digs in 1995 in the burgeoning Yerba Buena Arts District. In the stunning central **atrium**★★, lined with alternating bands of polished and unpolished black marble, you can climb the central staircase to the gallery floors. On the second floor, selections from the museum's permanent collection of more than 23,000 works illustrate the diversity of contemporary art. The third, fourth and fifth floors host special exhibitions.

If you're not afraid of heights, venture across the fifth floor's dramatic 35ft-long steel bowstring-truss **bridge**★ , suspended at a dizzying 75ft above the lobby. You'll find changing exhibits in a room at the other end.

Highlights of the Permanent Collection

Painting and Sculpture – Begin your introduction to this stellar group of 20C and 21C works with Matisse and move on to Picasso, Klee, Dalí, de Kooning, Motherwell, Rauschenberg and more.

Architecture and Design – Frequently rotating shows of furniture, graphic arts and building design are tapped from the permanent collection.

Photography – The museum's distinguished group of images dates from the 1840s to the present.

Edible Art

The museum's **Caffè Museo** *(415-357-4500; www.caffemuseo.com)* serves a Mediterranean-inspired menu for lunch—and for dinner on Thursday, when the museum is open late. The kitchen cooks up a different seasonal soup or stew every day; breads and pastries are baked on-site.

---

50   M I C H E L I N   M U S T   S E E S

National Maritime Museum★

[M⁶] *refers to map on front inside cover. Beach St. at Polk St. 415-561-7100. www.maritime.org. Open year-round daily 10am–5pm. Closed Jan 1, Thanksgiving Day & Dec 25.*

It's hard to mistake this big, white, ship-shaped building in the Fisherman's Wharf area. The 1939 Streamline Moderne-style museum, with its deck railings and porthole windows, looks just like an ocean liner berthed at the edge of the bay.

Part of the **San Francisco Maritime National Historical Park★**, the museum is located near the Hyde Street Pier historical ships that also fall under the park's umbrella. It was built as the Aquatic Park Casino, the intended centerpiece of a never-realized recreational complex built by the Works Progress Administra-

tion. Inside, be sure to take note of Hilaire Hiler's expressionistic undersea murals.

Go out on the upper deck for great **views★★** of the historical ships on Hyde Street Pier, the Golden Gate Bridge and the Marin Headlands.

Entrance Hall – You can't miss the giant ship's anchor, but search out the hull of a scow schooner and three

wonderful model ships, including the *Preussen*, a unique, five-masted German square-rigger. Elsewhere on the first level, exhibits detail the days of steam-powered ocean travel.

Second Floor – Displays here focus on fishing, whaling and shipbuilding in the 1850s and 60s, San Francisco's early years as a port. Blubber-processing spoons and intricately carved ships' figureheads number among the unusual artifacts.

Third Floor – Changing exhibits are showcased here.

The Buena Vista

2765 Hyde St. at the corner of Hyde & Beach Sts. 415-474-5044. www.thebuenavista.com. A short two-block walk east of the museum will bring you to a San Francisco institution: the **Buena Vista Cafe**. Known as the first bar in the US to serve Irish coffee (a heady concoction of Irish whiskey, coffee and whipped cream), this amiable bar sold its first steaming mug of brew in 1952. Go for a quick breakfast or lunch, or better yet, stop in after dinner for one of its signature spiked coffee drinks—the Buena Vista is open every day until 2am.

San Francisco Art Institute ★

800 Chestnut St., between Jones & Leavenworth Sts. 415-771-7020. www.sfai.edu. Gallery hours vary (see below).

A cultural center as well as a fine-arts college, the Art Institute was established in 1871 to foster understanding of contemporary art and to educate the leading artists of the time. The institute has attracted a wealth of forward thinkers in its time; alumni include Pulitzer Prize-winning cartoonist Rube Goldberg, painter Richard Diebenkorn, photographer Annie Liebovitz as well as the late Grateful Dead guitarist Jerry Garcia.

> **Art Institute Cafe**
> *415-749-4567. Closed weekends.*
> Wind your way through the art- and handbill-lined hallways to the institute's broad back deck. Grab a sandwich or a daily entrée—guaranteed to fill starving artists at rock-bottom prices—and sit back and relax. The foreground of congregating students against a stunning backdrop of city, bay and sky may inspire you to bring out your brushes.

Today the institute enrolls about 650 students and welcomes the public to its Spanish Colonial Revival-style campus near Russian Hill to view thought-provoking exhibits, attend lectures by local and visiting international artists, and watch the latest in avant-garde films.

Walter and McBean Galleries – *415-749-4563. Open year-round Mon–Sat 11am–6pm.* The school's main exhibition galleries showcase a year-round schedule of photographs, paintings, installations and other work by both local and international artists. The focus here is on newly commissioned art.

Diego Rivera Gallery – *415-771-7020, ext. 4410. Open year-round Mon–Sat 8am–9pm.* This chapel-like gallery features *The Making of a Fresco Showing the Building of a City* (1931) by the famed Mexican artist Diego Rivera (1886–1957). Rivera himself is pictured in the two-story mural, along with his wife, artist Frida Kahlo. Exhibitions of student work here change weekly. If you're in town on a Tuesday night, you might want to go by one of the opening receptions, which are free to the public *(every Tue 5:30pm–7:30pm).*

Wells Fargo History Museum ★

420 Montgomery St. 415-396-2619. www.wellsfargohistory.com. Open year-round Mon–Fri 9am–5pm. Closed major holidays.

Precursor to our modern-day overnight delivery services, Wells Fargo & Co. prided itself on its fast delivery of gold, mail and valuables when it was founded in 1852. Today the company operates as a bank, but in the company's museum you can relive the Old West days when villains like Black Bart robbed the stagecoaches. Kids will want to head straight for the mezzanine, where they can sit on a jostling reconstructed Concord coach and listen to a recorded description of a harrowing cross-country journey in the 1850s. Other exhibits tell the story of the Gold Rush days through photographs, letters, and glittering gold nuggets.

Museums at Fort Mason

At Fort Mason Center. Entrance on Marina Blvd. at Buchanan St. 415-345-7544. www.fortmason.org.

This former military base now houses a host of museums and galleries *(see Historic Sites).*

San Francisco Museum of Modern Art Artists Gallery – *Bldg. A. Open Sept–July Tue–Sat 11:30am–5:30pm. closed major holidays. 415-441-4777. www.sfmoma.org.* Sister to SF MOMA, the gallery displays rotating contemporary art exhibits and has given many local artists their start.

J. Porter Shaw Library – *Bldg. E. Open year-round Tue 1pm–8pm, Wed–Fri 1pm–5pm, Sat 10am–5pm. 415-561-7080. www.nps.gov/safr.* This maritime library features 32,000 books plus oral archives, sea chanteys, vessel registers, and photographs of West Coast shipping and whaling.

San Francisco African American Historical & Cultural Society – *Bldg. C. Open year-round Wed–Sun noon–5pm. $2. 415-441-0640.* The Society celebrates black culture through the visual arts and preserves African-American experiences.

Museo ItaloAmericano – *Bldg. C. Open year-round Wed–Sun noon–5pm. Closed major holidays. $3. 415-673-2200. www.museoitaloamericano.org.* A permanent collection of modern Italian and Italian-American art is featured here.

San Francisco Craft & Folk Art Museum – *Bldg. A. Open Tue–Sun 11am–5pm, Sat 10am–5pm. $4. 415-775-0991. www.mocfa.org.* Showcasing rotating exhibits of historical folk art and crafts from around the world, the museum also has a wonderful gift shop.

Parks and Gardens

When you begin to feel trapped by the city's concrete jungle, take a break at one of San Francisco's many parks and gardens. With its splendid location bordered by the ocean and bay, San Francisco claims some truly great areas for recreation. Oh, and be sure to wear a flower in your hair.

Golden Gate Park★★★

Bounded by Great Hwy. & Fulton St. and Lincoln Way & Stanyan St. 415-751-2766. www.parks.sfgov.org.

If you're old enough to remember the "Summer of Love" in 1967, Golden Gate Park probably brings to mind images of masses of tie-dyed-T-shirt-clad hippies and throbbing rock concerts in Speedway Meadow. A bit more low-key today, the 1,017-acre park now provides a place for residents and visitors—some 78,000 people each weekend—to escape the harried pace of the city.

Planning for Golden Gate Park began in the 1860's, when a land dispute with Mexico and fears that San Franciscans would eventually be overcrowded spurred city leaders to plan a park that would rival New York City's Central Park, already under construction. William Hammond Hall oversaw the daunting task of converting the sandy plot into a lush recreational area. When he retired, John McLaren took over as park superintendent; under his care, the area blossomed into Golden Gate Park as we know it today.

Recreation – The largest urban park in the US, Golden Gate offers 27mi of paths, 7.5mi of equestrian trails and provides fields for a wide variety of games, including baseball, tennis, golf and even petanque.

California Academy of Sciences★★

Closed until 2008. For details, see Museums.

Tips for Visiting Golden Gate Park

Stop for maps and information at the **Beach Chalet** visitor center *(415-751-2766; open year-round daily 9am–6pm)* or **McLaren Lodge** *(415-831-2700; open year-round Mon-Fri 8am–5pm)*. John F. Kennedy Dr. (north) and Martin Luther King, Jr. Dr. (south) form the park's two main thoroughfares. JFK Drive *(between Kezar Dr. & 19th Ave.)* closes to vehicular traffic Sundays and most holidays. On Saturdays, Middle Drive West closes south of the Polo field *(between 19th Ave. & MLK, Jr. Dr.)*. Parking is available throughout the park; disabled-parking spaces are located in the Music Concourse.

Japanese Tea Garden★★

Haigawa Tea Garden Dr. 415-752-4227. Open year-round daily 8:30am–5:30pm. $3.50.

If you need a meditative spot to relax after a long day of sightseeing, head to the serene Japanese Tea Garden. Here you can wander through five acres of meandering paths lined with azaleas, bonsai trees and rock gardens, and when you're ready, take a tea break at the open-air **teahouse** *(415-752-1171; open year-round daily 10am–5:15pm)*. If you're in town in April, be sure to see the spectacular display of cherry blossoms that paint the garden in pastel pink.

M. H. de Young Memorial Museum★★

On the Music Concourse in Golden Gate Park. Closed until 2005 for construction of new building. See Museums.

Strybing Arboretum★★

Martin Luther King, Jr. Dr. at 9th Ave. 415-661-1316. www.strybing.org. Open year-round Mon–Fri 8am–4:30pm, weekends & holidays 10am–5pm.

With 7,000 species of plants from all over the world represented in its 55 acres, the Strybing Arboretum is a must-see for any nature enthusiast. San Francisco's Mediterranean climate enables the arboretum to nurture plants from all over the world, including some that no longer grow in their native habitats. Walk through the Cloud Forest, where special mist machines supplement the San Francisco fog, wander the Redwood Nature Trail, or visit the Primitive Plant Garden, filled with cycads and horsetail ferns. Free guided walks are offered daily at 1:30pm.

Conservatory of Flowers★

Conservatory Dr. W. & JFK Dr. 415-666-7001. www.conservatoryofflowers.org. Open year-round Tue–Sun 9am–4:30pm. $5.

Colorful exhibits here are not only a joy to see, they teach visitors about current conservation efforts to save tropical habitats worldwide. Highlights include the steamy **lowland tropics**, home to the conservatory's most valuable plants; **aquatic plants**, where giant water lilies grow up to 5ft in diameter; and the lovely collection of orchids in **highland tropics**.

Children's Playground and Carrousel – *See Musts for Kids.*

San Francisco Shakespeare Festival

What's more lovely than a summer's day? Spending a fall afternoon watching Shakespeare in the Park! For some 20 years, the San Francisco Shakespeare Festival has been producing the Bard's works in Golden Gate Park (as well as locations in other Bay area cities), giving more than 50,000 people the opportunity to see a professional play free of charge. If you visit San Francisco between July and October, come see what all the ado is about. *For information: 415-865-4434 or www.sfshakes.org.*

Golden Gate National Recreation Area★★

Headquarters at Fort Mason, Bldg. 201, McArthur St. 415-561-4700. www.nps.gov/goga. Headquarters open year-round Mon–Fri 9am–5pm.

Encompassing many of the city's famous tourist attractions, along with 28mi of coastline and some stellar natural areas in its 75,000-plus acres, the mammoth Golden Gate National Recreation Area (GGNRA) is more than twice the size of San Francisco.

Established in 1972, the GGRNA harbors more than 1,250 historic structures, protects 27 endangered species, and preserves numerous threatened habitats in keeping with its lofty mission: "to preserve and enhance the natural environment and cultural resources of the coastal lands north and south of the Golden Gate for the inspiration, education, and recreation of people today and for future generations." As if that wasn't enough, the park also channels staff and volunteer efforts to establish educational programs such as its Parks as Classrooms initiative.

You probably won't have time to get to all of the GGRNA's different sites, but at the ones you do visit, spend the time to watch a sunset, take a walk, paddle a kayak or go camping. Each location offers something special, and whether you discover history, explore arts and culture, indulge in adventure or simply drink in natural beauty, you'll be sure to leave enriched by the experience.

The umbrella of the GGRNA covers a total of 34 different sites. Those listed below are described in this guide:

Alcatraz Island★★★
Angel Island★★
Cliff House★
Crissy Field
Fort Mason Center★
Fort Point National Historic Site★
Marin Headlands★★
Muir Beach

Muir Woods National Monument★★★
Ocean Beach★
Presidio of San Francisco★★
San Francisco Maritime National Historic Park★
San Francisco National Cemetery★
Stinson Beach★★
Sutro Bath Ruins★

Yerba Buena Gardens★★

Mission St. between Third & Fourth Sts., South of Market. See Neighborhoods.

Neighborhood Parks

Alta Plaza Park

Bounded by Jackson, Scott, Clay & Steiner Sts., Pacific Heights.

At the heart of the exclusive Pacific Heights neighborhood, Alta Plaza Park offers a great view of San Francisco's distinctive architecture, along with basketball and tennis courts and a children's playground. On the south side of the park, five staircases connect the U-shaped terraces John McLaren built to soften the hill's vertical slope. Today they provide excellent **views** of the city. Across from the terraces lie a famous series of elaborate Italianate Victorian houses (or "Painted Ladies") at **2637–2673 Clay Street**.

Buena Vista Park

Entrance at Haight & Baker Sts., Haight-Ashbury.

San Francisco's oldest park offers a glimpse of nature amid the counterculture of Haight-Ashbury. John McLaren, who was instrumental in landscaping both the Golden Gate and the Alta Plaza parks, had a hand in planning this one, too, in the early 1900s. If you're willing to brave the steep hill, you'll be rewarded with spectacular views of San Francisco's residential areas sweeping off to the blue waters of the bay.

Lafayette Park

Bound by Washington, Laguna, Gough & Sacramento Sts., Pacific Heights.

A four-block oasis with beautiful landscaping, Lafayette Park is a wonderful place to walk your dog or to stop for a picnic on a warm day. The park offers a number of walking paths as well as two tennis courts and a fenced-in playground. The northern edge of the park faces historic **Spreckels Mansion**★★ *(see Neighborhoods)*, currently owned by novelist Danielle Steel.

California Wine Merchant

2113 Chestnut St., near Steiner St., Pacific Heights. 415-567-0646. www.californiawinemerchant.com. For more than two decades, owners Greg and Deborah O'Flynn have traced the astonishing growth in popularity, variety and quality of California wines. Today their shop specializes in vintages from top-of-the-line small producers ranging from Napa Valley on up to Seattle. Their new location—around the corner from the original store—features a wine bar, with selections by the glass as well as a rotating schedule of wine tasting flights.

Historic Sites

San Francisco savors its long and baudy history. Thanks to public and private preservation efforts, you can glimpse the lives of the city's first settlers, honor the soldiers—Spanish, Mexican and American—who protected the city in times of war, and immerse yourself in the opulence of bygone days.

The Presidio★★

Access via Lincoln Blvd., Lombard St. (at Lyon St.), Presidio Blvd. (at Pacific St.) or Arguello Blvd. (at Pacific St.). 415-561-4323. www.nps.gov/prsf. For visitor center hours, see sidebar, below.

History with a view? You bet! Perched atop 1,480 acres overlooking the Golden Gate Bridge, the Presidio may be the most beautiful military installation in the US. The adobe quadrangle called the Presidio (Spanish for "military garrison") was built as a Spanish outpost in 1776, predating Mission Dolores by a month. Largely ignored by Spanish officials and plagued by decades of rain, earthquakes, wind and salt air, the fort was crumbling when the Mexicans acquired it from the Spanish in 1821. The US gained control of the Presidio in 1846, and four years later President Millard Fillmore issued an executive order to restore and expand the complex.

Tips for Visiting

Start your visit to this often fog-shrouded point at the **Presidio Visitor Center** on the Main Post *(50 Morago Ave., in the Presidio Officers' Club; open year-round daily 9am–5pm; closed Jan 1, Thanksgiving Day & Dec 25; 415-561-4323)*. Here you'll find museum displays on Presidio history, along with maps, walking-tour brochures and helpful park personnel.

As a US military installation, the Presidio protected California's silver and gold from Confederate troops during the Civil War and housed soldiers engaged in conflicts with western Indian tribes. After the devastating earthquake and fire of 1906, the fort's troops helped maintain order under martial law.

In 1962 the site was named a National Historic Landmark District. The Presidio's military career finally ended in 1994, when the fort was adopted by the National Park Service. Today the Presidio Trust, an official unit of the Golden Gate National Recreation Area (GGNRA), manages the Presidio with the goal of being completely self-sufficient by 2013.

Main Post★★

Heart of the Presidio, the Main Post is home to the fort's **visitor center** *(see sidebar p 58)* and a cornucopia of other sites and activities. Pershing Square, the former home site of General John "Black Jack" Pershing, anchors the southern end of the **Parade Grounds**. Nearby, a monument flanked by two 17C bronze cannons marks the location of the original Presidio compound.

Officers' Row★

One block east of the Parade Grounds, Funston Street was reserved for officers' housing. The Neoclassical and Italianate cottages on the row date from 1862 and 1863.

San Francisco National Military Cemetery★

Entrance off Sheridan St. at Lincoln Blvd. Since 1884, all US veterans have had the option of being buried in the Presidio's 28-acre burial ground. Animal lovers will be moved by the nearby **Pet Cemetery**, where headstones mark the graves of generations of beloved Presidio pets.

Coastal Defense Batteries★

From 1853 to 1910, a number of batteries were built between Fort Point and Baker Beach to protect San Francisco Bay from invasion by sea. Today they offer spectacular **views**★★★ of the sea, the Marin Headlands, and the Golden Gate Bridge. To enjoy the view, hike along the **Bay Trail** *(see p 60)* through the Presidio.

Baker Beach★

Bowley St., off Lincoln Ave. at the southwest corner of the Presidio. The smooth sands and high protective dunes of Baker Beach attract two types of beachgoers. The southern end, near the parking lot, draws families; the northern end, with its more dramatic view of the Golden Gate Bridge, is popular with nude sunbathers.

Crissy Field

Once a soggy marsh, Crissy Field was filled in for the 1915 Panama-Pacific International Exposition *(p 30)*, then paved four years later with 70 acres of asphalt as an Army aircraft test site. Today the area has come full circle, restored to its natural state as a tidal marsh, beach and dune environment. Strollers, picnickers, joggers and kite fliers share the broad, flat field with sailboarders, who on fine days raise their bright sails offshore on the wind-whipped waves. Overlooking the bay, **Crissy Field Center** focuses on environmental education *(Bldg. 603, corner of Mason & Halleck Sts.; open year-round Wed–Sun 9am–5pm; closed Mon, Tue & major holidays)*.

Fort Mason Center★

West of Fisherman's Wharf. Entrance on Marina Blvd. at Buchanan St. 415-345-7544.
www.fortmason.org.

On first glance, you might never think to stop at this complex of former military barracks, warehouses and docks. But look closer and you'll find myriad theaters, small museums, galleries, restaurants, and more than 40 non-profit organizations here.

Built on a landfill during the early 20C, Fort Mason was the official embarkation point for American troops and supplies being sent to the Pacific in World War II and the Korean conflict. During World War II alone, more than 1.5 million GIs and more than 23 million tons of cargo shipped from the fort's three docks.

The fort was decommissioned for civilian use in 1962, and the center was later transformed into a cultural complex for the community. Today this National Historic Landmark forms part of the Golden Gate National Recreation Area and serves as a fine example of a military facility that has been converted to peacetime use. More than 15,000 events are held here each year, ranging from folk art, music, and wine festivals to trade shows, dance performances and poetry readings.

Fort Mason Museums

See Museums.

Magic Theatre

At Fort Mason Center. See Performing Arts.

Greens Restaurant

At Fort Mason Center. Vegetarian cuisine with bay views. *See Must Eat.*

San Francisco Bay Trail

If you walk up to Fort Mason from the Fisherman's Wharf area, you'll notice cyclists and walkers following a path that hugs the shoreline behind the Maritime Museum. This is part of the Bay Trail, which when complete will surround the Bay Area with 400mi of jogging and biking paths. For now, only 240mi of the trail exist, but that should be more than enough to give you some exercise. From Fort Mason, you can follow the trail to the Golden Gate Bridge and walk across the bright orange span for some fantastic views of the city and the Marin Headlands. *For more information:* www.baytrail.abag.ca.gov.

Fort Point National Historic Site ★

Long Ave. & Marine Dr. Take Hwy. 101 North towards the Golden Gate Bridge, stay in the right lane and take the last San Francisco exit. Go through the parking lot to your right and turn left at Lincoln Blvd. Continue to Long Ave., which dead-ends at the fort. 415-556-1693. www.nps.gov/fopo. Open year-round Fri–Sun 10am–5pm until Golden Gate retrofitting is finished in 2007. Closed Mon–Thu and Jan 1, Thanksgiving Day & Dec 25.

When he first designed the Golden Gate Bridge, engineer Joseph Strauss planned to sink the southern anchorage at Fort Point, but after visiting the fort he was so impressed with its Civil War-era masonry that he decided to preserve it instead. Today Fort Point seems a lonely site, standing as it does beneath a massive steel arch of the bridge.

Fort Point in the Movies

The fort has been a backdrop for more movies than you'd ever guess. Here's a sampling:
Dark Passage (1947)
Vertigo (1958)
Point Blank (1967)
High Anxiety (1977)
Star Trek IV: The Voyage Home (1986)
The Presidio (1988)
Nine Months (1995)
When a Man Loves a Woman (1996)
Bicentennial Man (1999)

The fort was initially designed in 1861 as a simple rectangular granite structure, but was later modified to a full-scale brick fortress with defensive towers on the east and west. Fearing Confederate attack, soldiers rushed to occupy the fort before it was even finished. By the late 1800s, however, the development of faster, more powerful rifled cannons made this and other brick forts obsolete. The last cannon at Fort Point was removed in 1886.

From 1933 to 1937, the site served as base of operations for the Golden Gate Bridge build. The National Park Service restored and rebuilt Fort Point in the 1970s, and the fort now offers visitors a taste of late-19C military life on the California coast.

Exhibits – Three floors of displays range from the fort's history to the construction of the Golden Gate Bridge. Exhibits in the various soldiers' quarters depict life at Fort Point during the Civil War days.

Demonstrations, Tours & Videos – *Check listing at the Sallyport for daily programs.* Watch how soldiers loaded a Napoleon 12-pounder field cannon during the Civil War or take a 30-minute guided tour. There are also videos documenting the fort's history and the construction of the Golden Gate Bridge.

Mission Dolores ★

16th & Dolores Sts. 415-621-8203. www.missiondolores.citysearch.com. Open May–Oct daily 9am–4:30pm. Rest of the year daily 9am–4pm. Closed Jan 1, Easter Sunday, Thanksgiving Day & Dec 25. Suggested donation: $3.

"Dolores" means sorrow, and missing this lovely—and integral—piece of San Francisco's history would be sad indeed. The sixth mission in the Alta California chain, Mission Dolores was founded in 1776 near the present-day corner of Camp and Albion streets, two blocks east of its present site. Officially the Mission San Francisco de Asis, Mission Dolores is so-called for a nearby lake named after Our Lady of Sorrows.

The present chapel was completed in 1791, though illness among the neophytes (Native Americans who were newly converted to Christianity) impeded the mission's growth. By the time the mission was secularized in 1834, the neophytes had all but abandoned it. During the Gold Rush days, the area surrounding the mission became a haven for vice. The Catholic church reacquired the property in 1860 and enlarged the complex to accommodate its growing congregation. The present **church** ★ (1918) achieved basilica status in 1952.

Chapel ★★

This remarkably sturdy structure, with its 4ft-thick stucco walls, survived major earthquakes in 1868, 1906 and 1989. It is the oldest intact building in San Francisco, and thanks to a 1995 restoration program, it now appears as it did in 1791.

Cemetery ★

On the south side of the mission, you'll find this tranquil cemetery, where many of the city's early leaders, including Luis Antonio Arguello, the first governor of California under Mexican rule, and Francisco De Haro, San Francisco's first mayor, are buried. You'll recognize their names on streets nearby.

St. Francis Fountain

2801 124th St. at York St. 415-826-4200.
When you're in the Mission District, take a trip back in time with a visit to the city's only surviving soda fountain. Built in 1918, St. Francis Fountain recently reopened under new owners who are fixing the place up to look like it did in the good old days. Grab a stool at the counter and, if you dare, order a banana split royale. A heaping five scoops of ice cream with two toppings, whipped cream and, of course, a banana, this is one treat best shared with a friend.

Octagon House★

2645 Gough St. at Union St. 415-441-7512. Open Feb–Dec 2nd & 4th Thu & 2nd Sun noon–3pm. Closed Jan & major holidays.

These days many people use feng shui to create harmony and balance in their homes. In the 1860s, people built octagonal houses to improve their health. At the time, it was thought that this unusual floor plan allowed for more light and ventilation than that of an ordinary square-cornered house. Judge for yourself at the Colonial Dames Octagon House in Cow Hollow. Built in 1861, the house now serves as an art museum. The curious architecture is worth a trip in itself, but once inside you can admire the Colonial Dame's collection of early-American furniture, portraits, samplers, pewter and ceramics. History buffs will appreciate the room devoted to America's Founding Fathers; here, you'll find a collection of signatures and handwritten documents by all but two of the 56 signers of the Declaration of Independence.

Sutro Bath Ruins★

Access by foot off 1090 Point Lobos Ave. 415-239-2366. www.nps.gov/goga.

The raw, exposed ruins of Sutro Baths no longer evoke the grandeur they once represented. A gargantuan public swimming complex adjacent to **Cliff House★** *(see Musts for Fun)* the baths cost an estimated $1,000,000 to build in 1896. The complex was the brainchild of Prussian-born engineer Adolph Sutro, who struck it rich in Nevada's Comstock silver lode. Lupine and ice plants now cover the hills surrounding the baths' concrete foundation, and a tunnel once used to dump the dirt that collected in the baths pierces the bluff to the north. Follow the path above the tunnel to an **overlook**, where you can watch the waves crash off the rocky cliffs. Sea birds still bathe at the site but the water is brackish, the pools small.

Public Playground: The Sutro Baths

Millionaire Adolph Sutro's most beloved contribution to San Francisco was the Sutro Baths, a public swimming facility. Five cents paid for transportation to the pools on any one of three private railroads; a dime paid for admission to the complex; and for a mere quarter, visitors could swim. The freshwater pool and six saltwater pools—ranging in temperature from bathwater-warm to ocean-water-cold—were engineering marvels. Holding more than 1.5 million gallons of seawater, they could be filled or emptied by the tides in an hour.
Despite their popularity, the Sutro Baths were not commercially successful. Partly transformed into an ice-skating rink in 1937, the baths were eventually destroyed by fire, and the Golden Gate National Recreation Area incorporated the ruins in 1980.

Face it, there are some things that you *must* do while you're in San Francisco, no matter how touristy they are. So, come on and join the crowds riding the cable cars and photographing the crookedest street. At day's end, stop for a drink in one of the city's classic watering holes and take advantage of some eye-popping views. When all is said and done, you'll be glad you did.

Ride the Cable Cars★★★

Riding a cable car is a classic San Francisco experience, and something the whole family will enjoy. The city's celebrated open-air cable-car system provides access to many tourist attractions, notably Chinatown and Fisherman's Wharf. Today 40 cars climb San Francisco's hilly streets along three lines—Powell-Mason, Powell-Hyde and California Street—using the mechanism developed in 1873 by Andrew Hallidie *(see Museums; see Practical Information for details about how to ride)*.

Drive Down the "World's Crookedest Street"★★★

The one-lane brick-paved 1000 block of **Lombard Street**★★★ in the Russian Hill neighborhood takes eight—count 'em—unbelievably tight hairpin turns as it makes its way down from Hyde to Leavenworth Street *(see Landmarks)*. Drive it for yourself, or walk up the stairs that flank switchbacks filled with flower beds.

Take in the Best Views

Postcard Row★★★

710-720 Steiner St. between Hayes & Grove Sts.

One of the most photographed tableaux in the city, these seven pastel-painted Victorians—together nicknamed "Postcard Row"—appear pressed against a backdrop of twinkling skyscrapers. It's a trick of the landscape, of course; the slow uphill climb from the bay to Golden Gate Park makes the Financial District appear closer than it really is, almost as if the whole scene were being viewed through a zoom lens. **Alamo Square**★, banked up from the street on the west side of Steiner, allows photographers ample time to focus.

Twin Peaks★★★

From Haight St., drive south on Clayton St., cross Carmel St. and continue up Twin Peaks Blvd. to Christmas Tree Point parking area on the left; or take the No. 37 bus.

At 908ft (north peak) and 922ft (south peak), these twin summits offer panoramic **views**★★★ of the city and beyond. Brace yourself for large crowds, especially on summer weekends, and dress warmly; strong, cold winds are common year-round.

Catch a Giants Game at SBC Park★★

3rd & King Sts., at the Embarcadero. 415-972-2000. www.sfgiants.com.

Baseball fans won't want to miss the opportunity to see a game in this $319 million, 40,800-seat stadium (2000), which was designed to shield players and spectators from wind and fog. If you can't make a game, ball-park **tours** are held daily at 10:30am and 12:30pm *($10 adults, $5 children; 415-972-2400; no tours on game days).* During the 75-minute tour you'll get to visit the clubhouse, sit in the dugout and walk on the field. At the **Coca-Cola Fan Lot** *(on the Promenade level above the left-field bleachers)*, pint-size fans can slide into home plate through pop-bottle slides and run the bases at Little Giants Field.

Sunsets and Sea Lions at Cliff House★

1090 Point Lobos Ave., off 39th Ave. 415-386-3330. www.cliffhouse.com.

Ignore the busloads of tourists. **Cliff House★**, which hugs a high bluff above the Pacific Ocean in Sutro Heights, has long been a favorite spot to catch ocean breezes and stunning **views★★** up the rocky coast. Bring binoculars to spy on the raucous sea lions that roost offshore on **Seal Rocks** and stay to watch the sunset.

The third version of Cliff House (the first two were destroyed by fire) is now undergoing a $14 million renovation. Scheduled for completion in summer 2004, the project will add a two-level main dining room with ocean views, and a grand lobby to the 1909 structure (Cliff House remains open during the renovation).

Cocktails With A View

Drink in some of the city's best **views★★★** with your cocktail in two of Nob Hills's premier historic hotels: At the **Mark Hopkins Intercontinental Hotel** *(999 California St.; 415-392-3434; www.markhopkins.net)*, the **Top of the Mark** sky lounge has crowned the 19th floor since 1939. Go for a drink *(see Nightlife)*, a sunset dinner *(Fri & Sat)* or the Sunday buffet brunch.

Just across California Street at the **Fairmont Hotel★★** *(415-772-5000; www.fairmont.com)*, take the glass elevator to the 24th-floor **Crown Room** restaurant that tops the tower added to this property in 1961.

Surrounded by water and bordered on the north by the Marin Headlands (on the other side of the Golden Gate Bridge), San Francisco offers some great opportunities for recreation. Grab a bike or a pair of sneakers and exercise your heart out—just walking up and down the city's hilly streets is a workout in itself! If it's relaxation you crave, hop a cruise boat or just chill out at the beach.

Cruise the Bay★★

Getting out on the blue waters of San Francisco Bay makes a wonderful family excursion on a warm, sunny day and gives you a whole new perspective of the city skyline and the Golden Gate Bridge. Whether you just cruise the bay, sail under the bridge, or go to Alcatraz *(see Landmarks)* or Sausalito *(see Excursions)*, you can't beat the **views**★★★ from the water.

Tips for Cruising

Two major cruise lines, the **Blue and Gold Fleet** and the **Red and White Fleet**, both depart from piers at Fisherman's Wharf *(see Landmarks)*. Tours are narrated and last about an hour. In season, it's best to book in advance. Call or check the fleets' Web sites for schedules.

• Blue and Gold Fleet departs from Pier 41. 415-705-5555.
  www.blueandgoldfleet.com. $20 adults, $16 youth (age 12–17), $12 children (age 5–11).
• Red and White Fleet leaves from Pier 43 ½. 415-673-2900. *www.redandwhitefleet.com.*
  $20 adults, $12 youth (age 12–18), $9 children (age 5–11).

Walk the Coastal Trail★★

Trail starts at far end of the Merrie Way parking lot next to Cliff House (west end of Point Lobos Ave.). 415-561-4700. www.nps.gov/goga.

Part of the Golden Gate National Recreation Area, this 3.5mi loop trail makes for an invigorating walk along San Francisco's northwesternmost headland. On a clear day, the wild, heavily wooded shoreline here provides spectacular **views**★★★ of the ocean, the Golden Gate Bridge and the Marin Headlands. Eucalyptus trees scent the hills rising to the south, while Monterey pines and firs hold the crumbling cliffs in place with their gnarled roots. The winding main trail leads to a viewing platform overlooking the posh Sea Cliff neighborhood. The return route takes you through Lincoln Park Golf Course and past the California Palace of the Legion of Honor *(see Museums)* before ending at the Fort Miley parking lot.

Angel Island State Park★★

Access to the island is by private boat or public ferry from San Francisco. 415-435-5390. www.parks.ca.gov.

This hilly, forested island in San Francisco Bay served as a missile-launching base for the US military and as an immigration facility before it became part of the California state park system in 1963. Today you can explore the island by foot, by bike or by one-hour tram tour *(daily May–Oct; Mar, Apr & Nov weekends only; Angel Island TramTours; 415-897-0715; www.angelisland.com).* More adventurous souls can try the 2½-hour sea kayak tour *(Sea Trek Ocean Kayaking; 415-488-1000; www.seatrekkayak.com).*

Sandy unguarded beaches at **Quarry Point** and **Ayala Cove** (site of the park visitor center) are both good for picnicking and sunbathing (caution: swim at your own risk—currents are strong). From Ayala Cove you can access the 5mi **Perimeter Road** that loops around the island, and the rugged trail that climbs to the 781ft summit of **Mount Livermore**, where you'll have an unobstructed **panorama**★★★ of the Bay area.

Angel Island Ferry

The Angel Island Ferry is operated year-round by the Blue and Gold Fleet. The hop from Pier 41 on Fisherman's Wharf to Angel Island takes only 20 minutes *($12 adults, $6.50 children age 6–12; schedules: 415-705-5555 or www.blueandgoldfleet.com; no weekday service to the island in winter).*

Spend an Afternoon at Ocean Beach★

Although the chilling waters of the Pacific might not tempt you, the best option for beaching it in the city is the broad expanse of sand at **Ocean Beach**★, where San Francisco meets the sea. Part of the Golden Gate National Recreational Area, Ocean Beach extends from Cliff House *(end of Point Lobos Ave., off 39th Ave.)* 4mi south to Fort Funston. It's a great place to walk and jog—or sunbathe and picnic when it's not too windy—but swimming's not recommended in the rough surf (there are no lifeguards). Surfers are among the few who brave the dangerous riptides here. At **sunset**, park in lots along the Great Highway and watch the sun sink slowly in the west.

Y ou'd expect a city with such a free-wheeling spirit to love to play around. And San Francisco does just that—from the Pier 39 arcades to the zoo, kids of all ages—and young-at-heart adults—will find an ABCs full of fun in the City by the Bay. Here are a few of our favorites:

Golden Gate Park★★★ for Kids

Bounded by Fulton St., Lincoln Way, Stanyan St. & Great Hwy. 415-831-2700. www.parks.sfgov.org.

The park's 1,017 acres offer plenty of space for recreation, from ball fields to formal gardens. Several of its attractions will appeal particularly to children.

Steinhart Aquarium★ (California Academy of Sciences★★)

Temporarily located at 875 Howard St., between Fourth & Fifth Sts. The aquarium is closed to the public in Golden Gate Park until 2008 (see Museums). 415-750-7145. www.calacademy.org/aquarium. Open year-round daily 10am–5pm. $7 adults, $4.50 youth (age 12–17), $2 children (age 4–11).

The aquarium's temporary quarters near Yerba Buena Gardens hold some 5,000 animals, including black-footed penguins, a living coral reef and tanks full of fishes, snakes and frogs that represent the world's diverse underwater environments.

Exhibits have an inside-out design that allows you to peek behind the scenes, in case you've ever wondered about the mechanisms required to run an aquarium.

Children's Playground

East side of the park at Martin Luther King, Jr. Dr. & Bowling Green Dr.

Kids love to monkey around on the slides, swings and climbing structures here. Be sure to save time for a ride on the magnificently restored 1912 **carrousel★** *(below)*. Creative types can attend art classes in the 1888 Sharon Building, now the Sharon Arts Studio *(for schedules, call 415-753-7004).*

Carousels

Forget about thrill rides—who doesn't love an old-fashioned carousel? The 1912 Herschell-Spillman Company **Carrousel★** in **Golden Gate Park** was featured in the 1939 World's Fair on Treasure Island. It boasts a menagerie of 62 brightly painted wooden animals *(open Fri–Sun 10am–5pm; $1 adults, 25¢ children)*.

On the **Rooftop at Yerba Buena Gardens** you'll find a hand-carved carousel that was made in 1906. Its stable of 65 fanciful creatures is enclosed in a glass pavilion *(Fourth & Howard Sts.; open daily 10am–6pm; $2 for 2 rides)*.

The city's newest carousel, made in Italy, debuted at the north end of **Pier 39** in 2002 *(open Sun–Thu 10am–8pm, Fri & Sat 10am–9pm; $2)*.

Exploratorium★★

3601 Lyon St., at the Palace of Fine Arts (see Landmarks). 415-561-0399. www.exploratorium.edu. Open year-round Tue–Sun 10am–5pm. Closed Mon, Thanksgiving Day & Dec 25. $12 adults, $9.50 youth (ages 13–17), $8 children (ages 4–12). Free the first Wed of each month.

Science comes to life in hundreds of interactive stations inside the Palace of Fine Arts. By pushing buttons, rotating wheels, peering through prisms, and performing a host of other actions, you set experiments in motion and observe the results. Among the displays in physics, electricity, life science, weather, linguistics, sense perception and more, the **Seeing** and **Traits of Life** areas were both updated in 2002 to incorporate new research and revitalized exhibits. If you're not claustrophobic, try crawling through the multilevel **Tactile Dome**; inside it's pitch-black and soundproof, so you have to feel your way through.

Rooftop at Yerba Buena Gardens★★

Bounded by Mission, Folsom, Third & Fourth Sts. Entrances on Mission, Howard & Third Sts. 415-541-0312. www.yerbabuenagardens.com. Open year-round daily 6am–10pm.

At this two-block square urban park devoted to the younger set, kids can splash in a stream, romp in a 100,000sq ft children's garden, get lost in a hedge labyrinth, ice-skate year-round, go bowling, and ride a 1906 **carousel** *(see p 68)*—and that's just for starters.

Zeum★

415-777-2800. www.zeum.org. Open mid-Jun–Aug Tue–Sun 11am–5pm. Rest of the year Wed–Sun 11am–5pm. $7 adults, $5 youth (ages 4–18).

If you can dream it, you can do it at Zeum's 34,000sq ft production facility. Budding artists can draw, sculpt and paint; young animators can create flip-book or claymation cartoons; and little ones who crave the limelight can produce and star in their own videos.

Metreon—A Sony Entertainment Center★

[N] *refer to map on inside front cover. 101 Fourth St. at Yerba Buena Gardens. 415-369-6000 or 1-800-638-7366. www.metreon.com. Open year-round daily 10am–10pm.*

A four-level entertainment complex, Metreon combines game and play space with 15 movie theaters, an IMAX cinema, restaurants and shops. As for attractions with kid-appeal, there's the whimsical playspace, **Where the Wild Things Are** *(open daily 10am–6pm)*. Oversize monsters and other Wild Things from Maurice Sendak's popular children's book populate this fourth floor playground, where you can make your way through a maze of mirrors or visit the creepy goblin kitchen—just hope *you* don't end up being dinner!

Pier 39★

Beach St. at the Embarcadero.
415-981-7437. www.pier39.com.
Attractions & shops open year-round
daily 10am–8pm (hours vary season-
ally). See Neighborhoods.

Pier 39 packs oodles of entertainment for the whole family into
its festival marketplace. Be sure
to meet the resident "sea-lebri-
ties"—the noisy **sea lions**★ that hang out near K Dock *(free educational talks on
weekends, 11am–5pm)*.

Aquarium of the Bay★

*On the east side of the pier entrance. 888-732-3483. www.aquariumofthebay.com. Open
Jun–Sept daily 9am–8pm. Rest of the year Mon–Fri 10am–6pm, weekends 10am–7pm.
$12.95 adults, $6.50 children.*

Eels, octopi, sharks and other denizens
of the waters in and around San Francisco Bay will swim around you as you
walk through the clear tunnels on the
lower level of the three-story aquarium.
Some 23,000 aquatic animals from 235
different species are showcased here; at
three touch tables you'll have a chance
to meet some of them face-to-face.

More Fun on the Pier
But wait, there's more! For little ones there's the **carousel** *(see p 68)*; olders will get a
kick out of the virtual-reality **Turbo Ride** *($9 adults, $6 children 3-12)*. The whole family can star in their own movie courtesy of **Studio 39's Magic Carpet Ride** *(the ride is
free; the video costs $30)*. At the end of the pier, the **Riptide Arcade** features more
than 100 games, from the latest in virtual reality to an old-fashioned shooting gallery
(415-981-6300; www.riptidearcade.com).

San Francisco Zoo★

*Sloat Blvd. at 47th Ave. (vehicle entrance off the Great Hwy.). 415-753-7080.
www.sfzoo.org. Open year-round daily 10am–5pm. $10 adults, $7.50 youth (ages 12–17),
$4 children (age 2 & under free).*

What's new at the zoo? Lots of things. Since 1997 the San Francisco Zoo, which
perches on 125 acres overlooking the Pacific Ocean, has been in the process of
reinventing itself. Now boasting a new entrance, the **Lipman Family Lemur
Forest**, and the restored 1921 Dentzel carousel, the zoo plans to open its lush
African Savanna exhibit in mid-2004, and the hillside **Great Ape Forest** in
2005. Add to this such favorites as the **Primate Discovery Center**★, **Penguin
Island**, the **Australian Walkabout** and the six-acre **Children's Zoo** *(open daily
11am–4pm)*, and you've got a surefire prescription for fun.

Ghirardelli Chocolate Manufactory and Soda Fountain

Ghirardelli Square, 1st floor of Clock Tower Bldg., Larkin & North Point Sts. 415-771-4903. www.ghirardelli.com. Open year-round daily 10am–10:30pm (Fri & Sat until midnight).

It's always time for a hot fudge sundae—and what better place to get one than at the soda fountain of San Francisco's venerable chocolate maker? Located in the city since 1895, Ghirardelli satisfies sweet tooths with confections made with the company's yummy chocolate. Slurp a shake, lick a cone, sip a hot chocolate, but don't attempt the Earthquake—a gargantuan sundae with eight scoops, eight toppings, bananas, nuts and cherries—without reinforcements. Chocolate to go is available at the on-site store.

San Francisco Fire Engine Tours

Tours depart from the Cannery at Fisherman's Wharf (Beach St. at the foot of Columbus St.) year-round Wed–Mon at 1pm. 415-333-7077. www.fireenginetours.com. Reservations required. $30 adults, $25 teens (ages 13–17), $20 children.

A good time is guaranteed for all on this unique excursion. Put on your fireman's gear, board a 1955 Big Red Shiny Mack Fire Engine and join the crew in song! During the 75-minute sightseeing tour, you'll ride across the Golden Gate Bridge and stop at Fort Baker for a great photo op of the bright orange span.

Basic Brown Bear Factory★
2801 Leavenworth St., 2nd level of The Cannery. Open year-round daily 10am–5pm. Closed major holidays. 415-626-0781. www.basicbrownbear.com.
An entertaining guided tour *(daily every hour on the hour)* takes visitors behind the scenes to see how these cuddly teddies are made, from cutting the patterns to sewing the pieces together to blowing polyester stuffing into the bears. Kids can customize their own bear to take home—choose from 30 different styles and 80 different outfits.

Famed for its cultural diversity, San Francisco has always been a hotbed for performance. From a cappella to zydeco, you're sure to find something to suit your taste and pocketbook. Check local papers or *sfarts.org* for this week's events and critics' picks.

Music and Dance

San Francisco Ballet

War Memorial Opera House, 301 Van Ness Ave. (at Grove St). 415-865-2000. www.sfballet.org. Season: Feb–May.

The innovative ballet—the first professional company in the US—still ranks among the country's best, alongside New York City Ballet and American Ballet Theater. It is particularly acclaimed for its interpretations of works by George Balanchine.

San Francisco Opera

War Memorial Opera House, 301 Van Ness Ave. (at Grove St). 415-864-3330. http://sfopera.com. Season: Jun–July & Sept–Dec.

Of all the musical arts, opera is the one that has most enduringly won a place in San Francisco's heart. Decades before the city got a reputation for being "artsy," gold miners were getting an earful of Bellini. Today the company, widely recognized as the best on the West Coast, performs in the sumptuous War Memorial Opera House *(see Neighborhoods/Civic Center).*

San Francisco Symphony

Louise M. Davies Symphony Hall, 201 Van Ness Ave. 415-864-6000. www.sfsymphony.org. Season: Sept–July.

The appointment of the dashing young bachelor Michael Tilson Thomas as symphony director was hailed as the cultural event of 1995. An ardent champion of American composers, this Leonard Bernstein protégé has brought Aaron Copland, John Adams, Samuel Barber and, yes, Leonard Bernstein into the rotation, along with so-called "difficult" composers Gustav Mahler, Hector Berlioz and Rimsky-Korsakov.

Theater and Interdisciplinary Arts

Curran Theatre ★

445 Geary Blvd. 415-551-2000. www.currantheatre.com.

Producers Carole Shorenstein Hays and Scott E. Nederlander present their "Best of Broadway" series at the Curran, the Golden Gate Theater *(1 Taylor St.),* and the Orpheum Theatre *(1192 Market St.).* The fare consists of long-running musicals such as *Mamma Mia, Hairspray* and *The Lion King.*

Cheap Tickets

On a budget? Visit the **TIX Bay Area pavilion** in Union Square *(Powell St. between Geary & Post; closed Mon; 415-433-7827).* Here you can snag half-price tickets—most well under $30—to some of the finest drama and dance performances in the city. Go early for best availability.

Geary Theater★

415 Geary Blvd. 415-749-2228. http://act-sf.org.

This sumptuous 1909 landmark is home to the Actors Conservatory Theater (ACT), widely regarded as the best company in the city, with stellar performances and inventive stage sets. In a typical seven-play season, you're likely to see Charles Dickens' *A Christmas Carol*; works by well-known contemporary writers, such as William Saroyan; and world premieres of new works.

Zeum★

221 4th St., in Yerba Buena Gardens. 415-777-2800. www.zeum.org.

The 210-seat theater is used by ACT *(see Geary Theater, above)* for developing new works and staging small company productions, many with a multicultural focus.

Berkeley Repertory Theater

2025 Addison St., Berkeley. 510-845-4700. www.berkeleyrep.org. Season: Sept–July.

Winner of the 1997 Tony Award for the best regional theater in the US, the 36-year-old company puts on six to seven shows a season, a mix of classics and new plays.

Magic Theatre

Fort Mason, Building D. 415-441-8822. www.magictheatre.org.

Founded in a Berkeley bar in 1967 by director John Lion and a group of actors, the Magic is now situated in San Francisco's Marina District. It has a long history of introducing new works, including Sam Shepard's *True West, Fool for Love,* and Pulitzer Prize-winning *Buried Child,* as well as the first plays of Nilo Cruz, who won the 2003 Pulitzer.

Marines Memorial Theatre

609 Sutter St. 877-771-6900. www.marinesmemorialtheatre.com.

Long-running crowd-pleasers like Michael Frayn's *Noises Off* play at this historic 650-seat theater.

San Francisco Performances

Box office: 180 Redwood St. at Van Ness Ave. 415-398-6449. www.performances.org. Season: Sept–May.

For 24 years this group has been bringing the world's best singers, musicians, dancers and writers to the city for short-term engagements. Many of the season's 200 performances are staged at the Civic Center's Herbst Theatre.

Yerba Buena Center for the Arts Theater

701 Mission St. (at 3rd St). 415-978-2787. www.yerbabuenaarts.org.

Multiculturalism reigns at this new, 750-seat theater. Recent performances have included Chinese opera, African dance and new plays.

Must Shop

For all its anti-materialist pretensions, San Francisco is a terrific shopping city, catering to every taste and budget. You can get just about anything here if you know where to look, and looking is half the fun of it. In a city without a bad angle, shopkeepers know the virtue of stylish presentation.

The Cannery★★

2801 Leavenworth St. at Jefferson St. 415-771-3112. www.thecannery.com.

Built in 1907, this handsome brick building housed the most productive peach-canning operation in the world from 1916 to 1937. It was remodeled in 1968 as an airy, three-level retail and entertainment complex with a flower-filled sunken courtyard. Little ones will love the **Basic Brown Bear Factory**★, and **San Francisco Fire Engine Tours** depart right out front *(see Musts for Kids)*.

Ferry Building Marketplace★★

Embarcadero at Market St.

The soaring central arcade of the renovated 1898 **Ferry Building**★★ *(see Landmarks)* was recently transformed into a stunning showcase for the region's finest food.

Think artisan cheeses from Cow Girl Creamery, 50 flavors of hand-made gelato from Ciao Bella, 25 varieties of organic peaches from Frog Hollow Farm, and handmade bonbons from Recchiuti Confections. San Francisco City Guides give free 45-minute tours of the Ferry Building (samples included!) on Tuesday and weekends *(415-557-4266; www.sfcityguides.org)*.

Across the street, **Embarcadero Center**★ *(415-772-0700; www.embarcaderocenter.com)* holds more than 125 stores in a four-structure complex linked by pedestrian bridges.

Ferry Plaza Farmers' Market

At the Ferry Building. 415-291-3276. www.ferryplazafarmers market.com. Call or check Web site for schedules. This festive outdoor market operates year-round, drawing farmers, chefs and food lovers from all over the Bay Area. The large **Saturday market**★, which takes place on the rear plaza overlooking the bay *(8am–2pm)*, teems with tables heaped with organic produce (think white, red, and orange carrots; magenta-fleshed heirloom watermelon radishes), mouth-watering baked goods, fresh pasta and much more.

Ghirardelli Square★★

900 North Point St. between Polk, Larkin & Beach Sts. 415-775-5500. www.ghirardellisq.com.

Four decades after it spearheaded the revitalization of the waterfront, this 1864 chocolate factory still attracts flocks of visitors. Exposed brick walls and hardwood floors have been preserved throughout the interior, now packed with boutiques. Live music usually fills the central plaza, which is anchored by a mermaid fountain. Don't leave without sampling some goodies from the **Ghirardelli Chocolate Manufactory and Soda Fountain** *(see Musts for Kids)*.

Union Square★★

*Bounded by Sutter, Taylor,
Kearny & O'Farrell Sts.
www.unionsquareshop.com.*

San Francisco's ritziest retail
district centers on a palm-
and poppy-laden plaza,
where the city sponsors free
concerts and events
throughout the year. The
Westin St. Francis Hotel
looms over its western edge

(see Landmarks and Must Stay), and upscale department stores flank other
sides of the square: **Macy's West** and **Neiman Marcus** on the south side, and
Saks Fifth Avenue on the north. Well-heeled fashionistas flock to Union
Square in search of the perfect handbag, a couture ball gown, or a diamond
necklace. Even if you can't afford to buy, it's still fun to window-shop.

A Union Square Shopping Sampler

The list of chic shops surrounding Union Square reads like a who's who of big-name
designers:

Cartier – *231 Post St. 415-397-3180.
www.cartier.com.* French jewels for the very, very
well-to-do.

Gucci – *200 Stockton St. 415-392-2808.
www.gucci.com.* Brown and tan with G's all over,
the pimply leather of a Gucci bag is unmistakable.

Gump's – *135 Post St. 415-982-1616.
www.gumps.com.* The East-meets-West interior
design gallery has been a San Francisco fixture for
150 years.

Hermès of Paris – *125 Grant Ave. 415-391-7200.
www.hermes.com.* Elegant scarves, gloves and
leather goods, including saddles.

Napa Valley Winery Exchange – *415 Taylor St. 415-
771-2887. www.napavalleywineryex.com* Hard-to-
find vintages from you-guessed-where. Airline
carry-on packs and worldwide shipping available.

Wilkes Bashford – *375 Sutter St. 415-986-4380.
www.wilkesbashford.com.* This beloved local haberdashery has some of the most inventive window displays in the neighborhood. Antiques fill the basement.

Maiden Lane

Off Stockton St., between Geary & Post Sts.
Once lined by brothels, this charming street was reincarnated after the 1906 fire as a
quaint pedestrian lane. Today designer boutiques, salons and galleries fill its storefronts.

Best Neighborhoods for Shopping

Chinatown★★★

Grant Ave. between Bush & Jackson Sts.

Just north of the Chinatown Gate, **Grant Avenue**★★ explodes with shops selling trinkets, jewelry, artwork, electronics, bamboo and ceramics. The **China Trade Center** mall *(no. 838)* has three floors of additional stores. Stop at the **Chinatown Kite Shop** *(no. 717)* for brightly colored fish kites, box kites and windsocks.

Pacific Heights★

Fillmore St. between Jackson & Sutter Sts.

Hang on to your wallet. You could spend a full day and a lot of cash popping in and out of the scores of the interesting shops along Fillmore Street. Here, high-end thrift stores are sprinkled among the salons, cafes, antique shops and design stores, and women's clothiers.

Haight-Ashbury★

Haight St. from Central Ave. to Stanyan St.

Clothes and music are Haight Street's major exports. **Buffalo Exchange** *(1555 Haight St.; 415-431-7733; www.buffaloexchange.com)* does a brisk trade in quality used duds—from fancy-label chic to vintage originals. **Amoeba Music** *(1855 Haight St.; 415-831-1200; www.amoebamusic.com)* has a tremendous selection of new and used CDs, DVDs and vinyl.

Mission District★

Valencia St. between 16th & 20th Sts.

Rapid dot-commification in the 1990s brought a rash of eclectic boutiques to Valencia, along with a new generation of hipsters. Styles tend toward retro and vintage, sometimes veering into kitsch.

South of Market★

Bounded by Market, Duboce & Division Sts., and the Embarcadero.

This big area boasts a diverse mix of shopping. Near downtown, **San Francisco Shopping Centre★** *(865 Market St.; 415-512-6776)* is a nine-level mall, the top five floors of which are occupied by the tony department store **Nordstrom**. The **Old Navy** flagship *(801 Market at 4th St.; 415-344-0375; www.oldnavy.com)* stocks all manner of casual clothes. In **North Face Outlet** *(1325 Howard St. between 9th & 10th Sts.; 415-437-0100)* you'll find great deals on outerwear.

Cow Hollow

Union St. between Van Ness & Steiner Sts.

Despite its homely name—more than 30 dairy farms once occupied the site-Cow Hollow is just the opposite. Tree-lined Union Street's colorful Victorians house charming boutiques and restaurants, galleries, and bed-and-breakfast inns. Stop in **La Nouvelle Patisserie** *(2184 Union St.; 415-931-7655)* for a show-stopping lineup of French pastries.

Hayes Valley

Hayes St. from Franklin to Octavia St.

Just a stone's throw from City Hall, this once-sleepy strip has gotten funky of late, yet still caters to creatively minded locals. Boutiques sell one-of-a-kind glassware, pottery, jewelry, hand-painted clothing, antiques and art.

Japantown

Post St. between Laguna & Fillmore Sts.

Built in 1968, **Japan Center** anchors the small neighborhood of Nihonmachi, or Japantown. You'll find rice cookers, woks, origami paper, kimonos, lanterns, tatami mats, and all manner of animé DVDs in this three-block shopping arcade, as well as excellent restaurants, an art-house cinema, and a soothing spa *(see Must Be Pampered)*.

Bookstores

San Francisco has more bookstores per capita than any other city in the US. **City Lights★** *(261 Columbus Ave.; 415-362-8193; www.citylights.com)*, founded by beat poet Lawrence Ferlinghetti in 1953, remains a North Beach landmark for its extensive poetry collection and browser-friendly atmosphere. **A Clean, Well-Lighted Place for Books** *(601 Van Ness Ave.; 415-441-6670; www.bookstore.com)*, named after a Hemingway short story, anchors Civic Center—shop before or after the symphony, opera, or ballet; the store never closes before 11pm. Mergatroid, a wooden leprechaun, stands sentry outside **Green Apple** *(506 Clement St.; 415-387-2272; www.greenapplebooks.com)*, a sprawling warren of creaky-floored rooms piled floor-to-ceiling with used books. Mission District fixture **Modern Times** *(888 Valencia St.; 415-282-9246; www.mtbs.com)* stocks a huge selection of political books and academic titles.

Some folks might grumble about the relatively early last call at San Francisco's bars, but you don't hear many complaints about the quality and character of its establishments. Nearly every neighborhood has its local hangout, from Irish pubs to wine bars; of late, SoMa has exploded with clubs, some of which open late and rock till dawn.

Bars and Pubs

Bubble Lounge – *714 Montgomery St., Financial District. 415-434-4204. www.bubblelounge.com.* Flutes of cold bubbly can be sipped on satin couches and in overstuffed chairs at any of ten candlelit lounges.

Cafe du Nord – *2170 Market St., Castro District. 415-861-5016. www.cafedunord.com.* Mahogany and velvet dominate the decor at this swank former speakeasy, a magnet for young sophisticates.

Dalva – *3121 16th St., Mission District. 415-252-7740.* Reputed to have the best jukebox in town, this dim railroad flat of a bar celebrates happy hour each day from 4pm to 7pm with $2 pints, well drinks, and sangria.

Fuse – *493 Broadway, North Beach. 415-788-2706.* Locals love this North Beach newcomer, a cool blue lounge with creative cocktails and rocking DJs. Try the cucumber cosmopolitan.

Harvey's – *500 Castro St. at 18th St., Castro District. 415-431-4278.* This lively restaurant/bar at the heart of the Castro is named for Harvey Milk, an openly gay city supervisor who was murdered by his colleague Dan White in 1979.

Hayes and Vine – *377 Hayes St., Hayes Valley. 415-626-5301. www.hayesandvine.com.* The decor is muted, the music soft. The "menu" lists 40 wines by the glass and 500 by the bottle, but there's nary a wine snob on staff. Cleanse your palate with a plate of smoked trout.

Orbit Room – *1900 Market St., Castro District. 415-252-9525.* Retro rules at this sleek corner bar, where the service is friendly, the music is mellow (oldies, of course), and the cocktails are works of art. Don't be surprised to see a fleet of Vespas parked outside.

Owl Tree – *601 Post St., Union Square. 415-776-9344.* The Owl Tree attracts a flock of regulars thanks to its cheap beer, salty snacks and original decor: decorative owls are abundant, and wood paneling completes the look.

Specs' – *12 Adler St., North Beach. 415-421-4112.* Formally called Specs' Twelve Adler Museum Cafe, Richard "Specs" Simmons' maritime-themed hole-in-the-wall has local color (and locals) a-plenty.

Tonga Room – *Fairmont Hotel, California & Powell Sts., Nob Hill. 415-772-5278. www.tongaroom.com.* Thatched umbrellas hover over rustic tables and bedeck nearly all the drinks at this kitschy Polynesian bar, a Nob Hill institution with exploding volcanoes and an indoor lagoon.

Dance Clubs

Asia SF – *201 9th St., SoMa. 415-255-2742. www.asiasf.com.* You'll get a feel for San Francisco's wild nightlife at this bi-level club. Waitstaff at the second-floor cocktail lounge and Cal-Asian restaurant double as "gender illusionists" who periodically strut their stuff on a red runway. Below is a throbbing dance club.

Bambuddha Lounge – *601 Eddy St., Tenderloin. 415-885-5088. www.bambuddhalounge.com.* Intimate conversation nooks and a rocking dance floor, a heated poolside lounge and a cool circular bar—in other words, a little something for everyone. Wear black.

Elbo Room – *647 Valencia St., Mission District. 415-552-7788. www.elbo.com.* Reggae, hip-hop, jazz, and Brazilian bands set the crowd to dancing on the second floor of this popular Mission hangout. The cover is cheap *(under $10)*, and happy "hour" *($2 pints)* lasts from 5pm to 9pm daily.

Mezzanine – *444 Jessie St., SoMa. 415-820-9669.* No "hipper than thou" attitudes at this vast industrial space, where up to 900 souls have been known to crowd the dance floor at a time. The crowd is gay and straight; the DJs among the best.

111 Minna – *111 Minna St., SoMa. 415-974-1719. www.111minnagallery.com.* *$5 cover.* Qool, the long-running Wednesday-night happy hour at this funky art gallery/night club goes until 11pm and features up to six DJs spinning everything from drum-and-bass to progressive rock.

Ruby Skye – *420 Mason St. (between Geary & Post Sts.), Union Square. 415-693-0777. www.rubyskye.com.* Crowded, trendy and shamelessly posh, this over-the-top, Las Vegas-style club inhabits the old Stagecoach Theater. The Art Deco decor and dramatic lights make for a decadent scene. Dress up if you want to get in.

Ten15 Folsom – *1015 Folsom St. (between 6th & 7th Sts.), SoMa. 415-431-1200. www.1015.com.* Every big-name DJ in the world has spun here, at what some people believe is the most influential club on the West Coast. Buy tickets in advance for popular shows.

Cinephiles, Unite!

Clubs aren't your idea of fun? You're not alone. Thousands of the hippest hipsters in San Francisco flock to the movies, even on weekend nights. A good place to get your cine-fix is the 1,500-seat **Castro Theatre** ★ *(429 Castro St.; 415-621-6120; www.thecastrotheatre.com).* Decked out in gold leaf and velvet swag, this is a movie palace nonpareil. Foreign films, classics and rare oldies all make it to the mammoth screen here, as do new works from several annual film festivals.

Blues, Jazz, Rock and World Music

Bimbo's 365 Club – *1025 Columbus Ave., North Beach. 415-474-0365. www.bimbos365club.com.* They've been packing 'em in at this North Beach institution since 1951. The roster no longer includes jugglers, but you can still soak in the atmosphere, elegant decor and live music, from rockabilly to torch songs.

Biscuits & Blues – *401 Mason St., Union Square. 415-292-2853. www.biscuitsandbluessf.com.* Tasty Southern food and down-to-earth prices add to the appeal of this cool club, which gets some of the best blues acts around. Live music nightly.

Boom Boom Room – *1601 Fillmore St. 415-673-8000. www.boomboomblues.com.* Its intimate size and loyal following make John Lee Hooker's club near Japantown a draw for musicians and fans alike. Grooves nightly.

The Fillmore – *1805 Geary Blvd. 415-346-6000. www.thefillmore.com.* Impresario Bill Graham turned this 1920s dancehall near Japantown into a 1960s landmark by booking acts like Janis Joplin, Jimi Hendrix, and Jefferson Airplane. Today it's a haven for touring alternative rockers.

Great American Music Hall – *859 O'Farrell St., Tenderloin. 415-885-0750. www.musichallsf.com.* Soaring marble columns, an oak dance floor and an ornate wraparound balcony make this gorgeous 1907 nightclub one of the best places in town to see a show. The fare includes indie rock, and there's a full-service kitchen.

Lou's Pier 47 – *300 Jefferson St., Fisherman's Wharf. 415-771-5687. www.louspier47.com.* For those who think that the best places are tucked behind unmarked doors in obscure neighborhoods, take a look at Lou's. Right in the thick of Pier 39 mania, Lou's has been voted the best blues club in San Francisco time and again. Cajun food is served downstairs, music upstairs. Snag a window seat for a bay view.

Slim's – *333 11th St., SoMa. 415-255-0333. www.slims-sf.com.* Billed as the "home of roots music," this San Francisco institution, partially owned by rocker Boz Scaggs, has recently hosted the Psychedelic Furs, John Zorn, and the Knitters. The space is boxy and tends to be loud, so bring ear plugs—or buy them at the bar.

Yoshi's – *510 Embarcadero W. (Jack London Square), Oakland. 510-238-9200. www.yoshis.com.* The top venue for jazz in the Bay Area is, perhaps surprisingly, not in San Francisco—it's in a Japanese restaurant in Oakland. The cabaret-style theater, open nightly, presents world-class acts. Advance tickets are highly recommended.

Cabaret and Piano Bars

Harry Denton's Starlight Room – *Sir Francis Drake Hotel, 450 Powell St., Union Square. 415-395-8595. www.harrydenton.com.* Harry, the expansive proprietor, invites you to come for the views and stay for the entertainment at his ritzy rooftop nightclub. The four-piece Starlight Orchestra sets the crowd to dancing every Thursday to Saturday night *(reservations recommended).*

Plush Room – *York Hotel, 940 Sutter St., Union Square. 415-885-2800. www.plushroom.com.* This former 1920s speakeasy is your best bet for big-name cabaret (think Paula West and Jane Monheit). Every Friday after the show, the club presents the Va-Va-Voom Room, which bills itself as "the greatest burlesque show on earth."

Top of the Mark – *Intercontinental Mark Hopkins Hotel, One Nob Hill. 415-616-6916. www.topofthemark.com.* Perhaps the most famous bar in San Francisco offers 360-degree **views**★★★, perfectly poured martinis and a festive atmosphere. On Friday and Saturday nights, dance cheek to cheek to the music of the Black Market Jazz Orchestra. "Smart casual" dress code is enforced after 8:30pm.

Comedy Clubs

Cobb's Comedy Club – *915 Columbus Ave., North Beach. 415-928-4320. www.cobbscomedyclub.com. Closed Mon & Tue.* To take the stage at Cobb's you must have performed on *The Tonight Show with Jay Leno, Late Night with David Letterman, Conan O'Brien, HBO/Showtime Comedy Showcase,* or in a major feature film. Wednesday's "all-pro" comedy showcase is a great deal at $7.

Mock Cafe – *At the Marsh Theater. 1074 Valencia St. at 22nd St., Mission District. 415-826-5750, ext. 4. www.themarsh.org.* This laid-back, weekend-only comedy club carries on the Marsh Theater's mission of promoting new performers. Stand-up, improv and sketch comedy offered on Friday nights. On Saturdays catch the 10pm all-star showcase. No reservations.

Punch Line – *444 Battery St., 2nd floor, Financial District. 415-397-7573. www.punchlinecomedyclub.com.* The Punch Line draws the funniest of the funny: Robin Williams, Ellen Degeneres, Rosie O'Donnell, Drew Carey, Chris Rock and Dana Carvey have all crossed the stage here. Today, the club hosts the likes of Margaret Cho, Dave Chappelle and Jay Mohr.

Beach Blanket Babylon

Club Fugazi, 678 Beach Blanket Babylon St. (formerly Green St.), North Beach. 415-421-4222. www.beachblanketbabylon.com. Where else can you find Paris Hilton and Oprah Winfrey, Martha Stewart and Arnold Schwarzenegger, J.Lo and Eminem—and some of the most ludicrous hats ever created—together on the same stage? This outrageous spoof of current events and pop culture has played before packed houses eight times weekly since 1974, when it was hatched by impresario Steve Silver. It is acclaimed as the longest-running musical review in history.

Must Be Pampered: Spas

Even the hardiest traveler needs a break from all those hills. Spas to the rescue. The following spas provide everything from a quick dip in the hot tub to a luxurious day of self-centered bliss, from scalp massage to pedicure.

International Orange Spa Yoga Lounge

2044 Fillmore St. (2nd floor), Pacific Heights. 415-563-5000. www.internationalorange.com.

Health- and body-conscious San Franciscans rave about the aromatherapy deep-tissue massages at this stylish newcomer, owned and operated by three young women. The key here is relaxation. Enjoy fruit and cheese on the sunny back deck. Throw in a yoga class and you'll understand what they mean by "the essence of wellness."

Spa Claremont

41 Tunnel Rd., Berkeley. 510-843-3000 or 800-551-7266. www.claremontresort.com.

Buy a spa package at this historic Berkeley resort complex—it's been open since 1915—and you basically get the run of the place for a day: health club, lounge, outdoor swimming pools, steam room, sauna and fitness classes—all yours to enjoy. That's on top of your individualized treatments: massages, facials, manicures, pedicures. Lunch is included. Come on a weekday, when prices are lower and the facilities are less crowded.

Kabuki Springs & Spa

1750 Geary Blvd. (at Fillmore St.), Japantown. 415-922-6002. www.kabukisprings.com.

A sojourn in this day spa will revive even the most bone-tired traveler. Soak in the traditional Japanese baths and enjoy a full range of modern spa treatments, including ayurvedic rebalancing and seaweed wraps. Shiatsu massage is a specialty.

Mister Lee Beauty, Hair and Health Spa

834 Jones St. between Bush and Sutter Sts., Union Square. 415-474-6002. www.misterlee.com.

Tucked away on the third floor, this spa sports an Egyptian theme. Follow up an aromatic hydrotherapy soak—the whirlpool here has 70 pressurized jets—with a hot-stone massage or facial. If you're crunched for time, try the 90-minute sampler package, which includes the tub treatment; a facial; a hand, shoulder, neck and scalp massage; and a shampoo and blow dry.

Nob Hill Spa

1075 California St., in the Huntington Hotel, Nob Hill. 415-345-2888. www.huntingtonhotel.com.

This 11,000sq ft sanctuary urges guests to reconnect with the gentle life. The pool, Jacuzzi and saunas will be at your disposal. Pilates and other fitness classes are offered. Treat-

ments include packages promoting longevity (six hours of full-body treatments, including lunch); serenity (three hours of spa access, plus a massage or facial), and harmony (a romantic night of side-by-side massages, followed by a candlelight dinner catered by the hotel's **Big Four** restaurant).

Novella Spa and Imports

2238 Union St., Cow Hollow. 415-673-1929. www.novellasalon.citysearch.com.

Indonesian accents will put you in an island mood—just the thing to enjoy a "Javanese beauty ritual" that comprises massage, exfoliation and body-wrapping. The aromatic salts and oils used throughout the process are transporting. Come with a friend Wednesday and Thursday before 4pm and get one of your $85-and-up treatments for half price.

77 Maiden Lane Salon and Spa

77 Maiden Lane (Suite 2), Union Square. 415-391-7777. www.77maidenlane.com.

Though it's a favorite among style-conscious celebrities, 77 Maiden Lane doesn't have the uppity pretenses of some high-end spas. The aim here is to make you look and feel gorgeous. For the travel weary, a short, simple massage might do the trick—prices are surprisingly reasonable. Luxury packages run four to eight hours and include a bit of everything: mud bath, massage, loofah scrub, pedicure, manicure, hair cut/color, makeup, or some combination thereof. There's even a "tune-up" for men.

Wine Country Spas

Relaxing just seems to go hand-in-hand with the slower pace of life in the Wine Country. From luxe facilities in Napa and Sonoma to Calistoga's mineral and mud baths *(see Excursions/Wine Country)*, there's a treatment to suit every sore muscle.

Fairmont Mission Inn and Spa – *18140 Sonoma Hwy. (Rte. 12), Sonoma. 707-938-9000 or 866-540-4499. www.sonomamissioninn.com.* The bathing ritual is the thing to do at this Fairmont spa, which boasts it own source of thermal mineral water. Begin with an exfoliating shower, climb into a warm mineral bath (98°F), then into a hot mineral bath (102°F), and finish with a cool shower.

Meadowood – *900 Meadowood Lane, St. Helena. 707-967-1275. www.meadowood.com.* The luxurious full-service resort *(see Must Stay/Wine Country)* offers a separate spa with a pool, fitness classes, personal training and yoga instruction. If the thought of working out is too much for you, indulge in a Cascading Stone Massage, in which two therapists work in tandem massaging your body with warm and cool stones.

Spa du Soleil – *180 Rutherford Hill Rd., Rutherford. 866-228-2490. www.aubergedusoleil.com.* Occupying a 7,000sq ft stucco building at the upscale Auberge du Soleil *(see Must Stay/Wine Country)*, the spa incorporates the local harvest in its treatments. Try a warm grapeseed oil massage or perhaps an olive-leaf body exfoliation.

Villagio – *6481 Washington St., Yountville. 707-944-8877 or 800-351-1133. www.villagio.com.* Balance your body, mind and spirit in the Mediterranean-inspired spa at the Villagio Inn. Two-hour-plus "spa experiences," named for the elements— water, earth, fire, air—are designed to promote wellness.

Although you may be justifiably hesitant to leave San Francisco, within a two-hour drive of the city you'll find ancient stands of redwoods and windswept beaches, the intellectual hub of Berkeley and the charming sun-washed towns of Monterey and Carmel, not to mention the world-renowned Wine Country. With all this to choose from, your most difficult decision will be where to start!

Muir Woods National Monument★★★

17mi north of San Francisco. Take US-101 north to the Hwy. 1/Muir Woods exit and follow signs. 415-388-2596. www.nps.gov/muwo. Open year-round daily 8am–dusk. $3.

"This is the best tree-lovers monument that could possibly be found in all the forests of the world," claimed legendary conservationist **John Muir** (1838–1914) when describing the national monument named for him. Located in an area that was difficult for loggers to access, Muir Woods managed to escape the lumbermen's saws in the mid-19C and eventually became a national monument, largely through the efforts of Congressman William Kent and his wife, Elizabeth, who donated the land. Some of the awe-inspiring trees in Muir Woods are as tall as 36-story buildings and date back more than 1,000 years.

Visit – Begin at the **visitor center** (*open year-round daily 9am–dusk*) to buy trail maps, attend a nature lecture or take a guided tour. The paved 1mi **Main Trail** will introduce you to a mature redwood forest, including the primitive plants, such as cycads and horsetail ferns, which continue to grow in the understory. You can see Muir Woods' most impressive trees in **Cathedral Grove** and **Bohemian Grove**, site of the park's tallest tree.

Muir Beach Overlook

2.5mi east of Muir Woods; go north on Hyw. 1.

While you're in the area, stop by this overlook off Highway 1, where a platform above the cliffs will give you stunning **views**★★ of the coast. Nearby **Stinson Beach**★★ *(5mi north of Muir Beach Overlook)* is a great place to swim and picnic.

John Muir

Years before we dealt with the thorny political issues of pollution and development encroaching on natural areas, John Muir warned: "If the importance of forests were at all understood, even from an economic standpoint, their preservation would call forth the most watchful attention of government." Not only did Muir establish the Sierra Club, but he also played a role in the creation of the Grand Canyon, Sequoia and Kings Canyon, and Mt. Rainier national parks. Today Muir Woods honors the great conservationist's legacy.

Wine Country★★★

Picnicking on artisan cheeses and fresh crusty bread amid acres of gnarled grapevines. Sipping wine on a terrace above a hillside of silvery olive trees. Touring caves heady with the sweet smell of fermenting grapes. This is the Wine Country. From the renowned Napa Valley west to the Sonoma Valley and north to the Russian River Valley, Northern California's Wine Country creates a feast for the senses that would make Bacchus (the Roman god of wine) envious. Lying inland within an hour's drive north of San Francisco, Napa Valley and Sonoma County thrive on the abundant sunshine and fertile soil that produce grapes for some of North America's finest wines. Differences in elevation, proximity to the sea and exposure to sun, fog and wind create myriad microclimates, each affected by factors as seemingly insignificant as a dip in a mountain ridge or the tilt of a slope. The first wineries were established in northern California in the late 19C. In recent decades the Wine Country has exploded into a center not only for wine, but for fine art, gastronomy and tourism.

Tips for Visiting Wine Country

Go in spring when the mustard plants turn the vineyards yellow, or in fall—the more crowded season—to see the harvest. Contact the following agencies for information:

Napa Valley Conference & Visitors Bureau – *1310 Napa Town Center, Napa. 707-226-7458. www.napavalley.com.*

Sonoma Valley Visitors Bureau – *453 1st St. E., Sonoma. 707-996-1090. www.sonomavalley.com.*

Sonoma County Tourism Information – *520 Mendocino Ave., Santa Rosa. 707-565-5385. www.sonoma.com.*

Russian River Valley Chamber of Commerce & Visitor Center *16209 1st St., Guerneville. 707-869-9000. www.russianriver.com.*

Russian River Wine Roads – *800-723-6336. www.wineroad.com.*

Recreation

Napa Valley Wine Train *(707-253-2111 or 800-427-4124. www.winetrain.com)* takes passengers on a 3-hour, 36mi tour of the Wine Country from Napa to St. Helena. Relax aboard vintage 1910 train cars as you ride through breathtaking scenery.

Ballooning – Up, up and away! If you want to see the Wine Country from above, consider a balloon tour: **Above the Wine Country** *(707-829-9850; www.balloontours.com)*, **Adventures Aloft** *(707-944-4408 or 800-944-4408; www.nvaloft.com)*, **Aerostat Adventures** *(707-433-3777; www.aerostatadventures.com)*, and **Bonaventura Balloon Company** *(707-944-2822 or 800-359-6272; www.bonaventureballoons.com)*.

Biking is a great way to enjoy the Wine Country. **Wine Country Bikes** *(707-545-7960; www.winecountrybikes.com)* and **Get-Away Adventures** *(707-763-3040; www.getawayadventures.com)* provide rentals and tours through the area.

Napa Valley★★★

41mi northeast of San Francisco via I-80 East and Rte. 29 North. For visitor information, see p 85. Sights in the Napa Valley are described from south to north.

Cradled between two elongated mountain ranges, this world-renowned valley extends about 35mi from San Pablo Bay northwest to Mount St. Helena. Many of California's most prestigious wineries cluster along traffic-choked Route 29—the St. Helena Highway—as it passes through the towns of **Napa**, **Yountville**★, **Oakville**, **Rutherford**, **St. Helena**★ and **Calistoga**★. Others dot the more tranquil **Silverado Trail**★, which parallels Route 29 to the east.

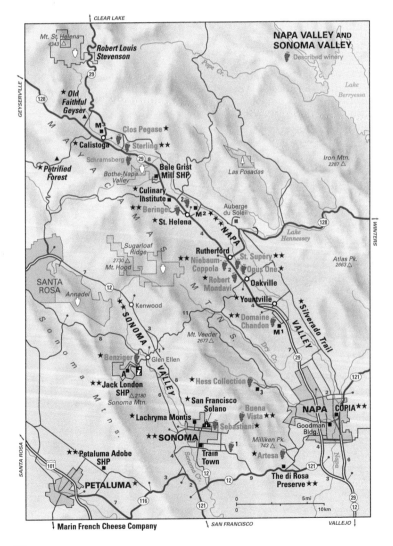

COPIA: The American Center for Wine, Food and the Arts ★★

500 1st St., between Soscol Ave. & Silverado Trail, Napa. 707-259-1600. www.copia.org. Open year-round Wed–Mon 10am–5pm. Closed Tue, Jan 1, Thanksgiving Day & Dec 2425. $12.50 (half-price on Wed).

You can easily spend half a day in this $70-million cultural and educational center founded by wine-maker Robert Mondavi (hardcore foodies will want to spend the whole day). Here professional chefs, winemakers and artists share their passions through a changing schedule of daily lectures (food traditions,

nutrition, food and beauty), cooking demonstrations, classes, tours and wine-tastings *(free with admission)*. The core exhibit, **Forks in the Road** *(2nd floor)*, takes a playful look at American culture through food and drink. Elsewhere in the museum, changing displays run the gamut from food in fashion to the art of cake decoration. On the first floor, **Cornucopia** is a shopper's wonderland of cookbooks, tableware, linens, cookware and private-label wines. Outside, five acres of garden plots showcase edible plants and teach organic gardening techniques.

Julia's Kitchen

Call or check Web site for hours. Reservations recommended. 707-265-5700. www.copia.org. When all those food demos have piqued your appetite, savor a leisurely lunch or dinner at **Julia's Kitchen**, named for the doyenne of French food in America, Julia Child. California-French dishes here incorporate ingredients hand-picked from COPIA's bountiful gardens.

di Rosa Preserve ★★

5200 Carneros Hwy./Rte. 121 (2.5mi west of Rte. 12). Visit by guided tour only; reservations required. Call for tour times: 707-226-5991. www.dirosapreserve.org. $12 (free admission the 1st & 3rd Wed of each month).

The two-and-a-half-hour guided tour of this 1886 stone winery showcases the art collection of René di Rosa, son of a US ambassador to Italy who came to San Francisco from Yale University in the 1950s as a young newspaper reporter. In 1960 he purchased 460 acres of abandoned vineyards in the Carneros area of lower Napa Valley, converting the winery into his home. Over the years he amassed a personal collection of more than 1,500 works—produced in the greater San Francisco area in the last half of the 20C.

Napa Valley Museum ★

[M¹] *refer to map p 86. 55 Presidents Circle, Yountville. Open year-round Wed–Mon 10am–5pm. Closed Tue, Jan 1, Thanksgiving Day & Dec 25. $4.50. 707-944-0500. www.napavalleymuseum.org.*

If you're perplexed by the winemaking process, the museum's multimedia display, **California Wine: The Science of an Art ★★**, will clear things up for you. By means of a computerized, interactive audiovisual program, you can experience a full year in Napa Valley winemaking, exploring soils, microclimates, grape growth, rootstocks, pests, varietal characteristics, and the winemaking process itself from harvest to bottling. An upper gallery features **The Land and People of the Napa Valley**, which describes the region's cultural and environmental heritage.

> ### Oakville Grocery
>
> *7856 St. Helena Hwy./Rte. 29, Oakville. 707-944-8802. www.oakvillegrocery.com.* Smoked-duck pâté, white peach preserves, more than a dozen types of olives, an impressive array of local vintages, and the best-stocked cheese counter in Napa Valley make this tiny but deliciously crammed grocery a must-stop for picnic or pantry supplies.

Robert Louis Stevenson Silverado Museum ★

[M²] *refer to map p 86. 1490 Library Lane, St. Helena. Off Main St./Rte. 29. Open year-round Tue–Sun noon–4pm. Closed Mon & major holidays. 707-963-3757. www.westerni.unibg.it/rls/museums.htm.*

Located in a pleasant gallery within the town library building, this small, densely packed museum is devoted to the life and works of Robert Louis Stevenson (1850–1894), author of such tales as *Treasure Island* and *Kidnapped*.

Culinary Institute of America at Greystone ★

2555 Main St. (Rte. 29), north of downtown St. Helena. www.ciachef.edu.

The massive stone building, erected in 1889 as Greystone Cellars, now houses the West Coast campus of the renowned Culinary Institute of America (CIA). Visitors are welcome to view the whimsical collection of more than 1,800 corkscrews, attend daily cooking demonstrations *(reservations: 707-956-2320)*, or browse through the **Spice Island Marketplace**, stocked with kitchen equipment, tableware, linens, and shelves upon shelves of cookbooks. Make reservations for lunch or dinner in the acclaimed **Wine Spectator Greystone Restaurant**, where you can watch professional-chefs-in-training prepare your meal in the open kitchen.

Sharpsteen Museum ★

[M³] *refer to map p 86. 1311 Washington St., Calistoga. Open daily 11am–4pm. Closed Thanksgiving Day & Dec 25. $3. 707-942-5911. www.sharpsteen-museum.org.*

Founded in 1979 by Ben Sharpsteen—one of Walt Disney's original 11 animators and later an Oscar-winning producer—this small museum contains an intriguing group of miniature dioramas re-creating scenes from Calistoga's colorful past.

Old Faithful Geyser ★

From Route 29 heading north, turn left on Tubbs Lane in Calistoga. Open year-round daily 9am–6pm. $8. 707-942-6463. www.oldfaithfulgeyser.com.

If you'd like to see one of the area's geysers for yourself, come to the foot of Mount St. Helena. This privately owned geyser is one of the world's three known "faithful" geysers, so called for their regular eruptions (the others are in Yellowstone National Park and in New Zealand). Approximately every 14 minutes, the geyser spews a column of superheated water 60 to 100ft into the air.

Petrified Forest ★

6mi west of Calistoga via Rte. 128 North. Open Jun–Sept daily 9am–6pm. Rest of the year daily 9am–5pm. Closed Thanksgiving Day & Dec 25. $5. 707-942-6667. www.petrifiedforest.org.

A circuit trail through this small, privately owned forest winds past the remnants of fallen giant redwoods turned to stone more than three million years ago when Mount St. Helena erupted and covered the surrounding area with ash and molten lava. Among the highlights is **The Giant**, an ancient redwood measuring 60ft long and 6ft in diameter.

Mud Baths and Mineral Springs

Volcanic activity in the northern Napa Valley has erupted in a multitude of geysers and hot springs, many of which have been harnessed to fuel the famed spas of **Calistoga ★**. Founded in 1859, this resort hamlet hunkers in the shadow of Mount St. Helena (4,343ft) where tourists flocked—both then and now—to experience the health-promoting power of the local waters.

Today you can get an hour-long basic mud-bath package, including mud bath, herbal wrap and mineral whirlpool bath, for $50 to $70; massages, facials and mineral-pool soaks will cost you extra. The Calistoga Chamber of Commerce *(1458 Lincoln Ave., Calistoga; 707-942-6333; www.calistogachamber.com)* can provide a list of spas in the area. Here are some places to start:

Calistoga Spa Hot Springs – *1006 Washington St. 707-942-6269. www.calistogaspa.com.*
Calistoga Village Inn and Spa – *1880 Lincoln Ave. 707-942-0991. www.greatspa.com.*
Dr. Wilkinson's Hot Springs Resort – *1507 Lincoln Ave. 707-942-4102. www.drwilkinson.com.*
Golden Haven Spa & Resort – *1713 Lake St. 707-942-6793. www.goldenhaven.com.*
Mount View Hotel & Spa – *1457 Lincoln Ave. 707-942-6877. www.mountviewspa.com.*

Sonoma County★★

The town of Sonoma is 49mi north of San Francisco via US-101 north to Rte. 37 East to Rte. 121/12. For visitor information, see p85.

Enjoying a reputation for excellent produce and other farm products, as well as for wines, Sonoma County incorporates the diverse viticultural areas of the Sonoma Valley, the Russian River Valley, the Dry Creek Valley and the Alexander Valley. In the southern portion of the county, the historic town of **Sonoma** dominates the **Sonoma Valley★★**, which parallels Napa Valley on the west side of the Mayacamas Mountains. In the northern end of Sonoma County, the **Russian River Valley★** follows the curving path of its namesake river as it meanders south through the town of **Healdsburg★** and veers west to the coast. Known for its Zinfandel wines, the delightful **Dry Creek Valley★** extends from Lake Sonoma to just south of Healdsburg; the neighboring **Alexander Valley★** centers along Route 128 northeast of Healdsburg *(tourist information: Healdsburg Area Chamber of Commerce: 217 Healdsburg Ave.; 707-433-6935; www.healdsburg.org).*

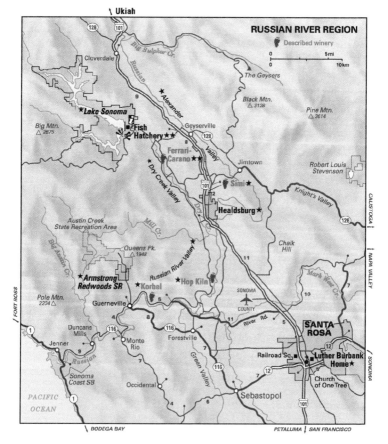

Sonoma★★

Site of California's northernmost and final mission, this charming community is the Wine Country's most historically significant town. It was born as the site of the San Francisco Solano Mission *(below)* in 1823 and retains its historic flavor, even though many of its venerable adobe buildings are now occupied by shops, restaurants and inns.

Sonoma's eight-acre central **plaza**★ *(bounded by Spain St., Napa St. & 1st Sts. W. & E.)* was the scene, on June 14, 1846, of the **Bear Flag Revolt**, an uprising of American settlers desirous of US control of California. Hoisting a white flag emblazoned with a brown bear and a star, the group proclaimed California an independent republic. The following month, American forces captured Monterey, declared California a US possession, and effectively ended the short-lived republic. Near the plaza's northeast corner, a bronze statue of a soldier raising the Bear Flag commemorates the revolt.

Sonoma State Historic Park★★

Sites open year-round daily 10am–5pm. Closed Jan 1, Thanksgiving Day & Dec 25. $2 for all sights (tickets available at any of the three park sights below). www.parks.ca.gov.

Around the plaza stand an array of buildings now open to the public under the auspices of the state historic park. Across First Street from the plaza, **San Francisco Solano Mission**★ *(corner of E. Spain St. & 1st St. E.; 707-938-9560)* was established in 1823 by Padre José Altamira to help solidify Mexican holdings against invasion. All that remains of the mission complex are the restored chapel and part of the priests' quarters.

Overlooking the plaza, the two-story adobe **Sonoma Barracks**★ was built in 1841 *(across 1st St. E. from the mission; 707-938-9420)*. The barracks once housed Mexican troops who guarded the new pueblo; today it contains artifacts from the various periods of Mexican and American settlement.

Nearby, the final home of **General Mariano Vallejo** (1807–1890) was named **Lachryma Montis**★, or "tear of the mountain" in Latin, for the mountain spring on the property *(.5mi from Plaza on 3rd St. W.; 707-938-9559)*. Vallejo was called by Mexican governor Figueroa to oversee the secularization of the Sonoma mission and the founding of a defense outpost there. Appointed commander of all Mexican troops in California in 1835, Vallejo was elected to California's first state senate in 1850. His home's airy interior paints a delightful picture of the general's genteel lifestyle.

Jack London State Historic Park★★

10mi northwest of Sonoma at 2400 London Ranch Rd., Glen Ellen. Open year-round daily 10am–5pm. Closed Jan 1, Thanksgiving Day & Dec 25. $8/car. 707-938-5216. www.jacklondonpark.com.

Sprawling among peaceful hills in the shadow of Sonoma Mountain, 800-acre "Beauty Ranch" was home to author Jack London (1876–1916) and his second wife, Charmain. In 1911 the couple began construction of a four-story mansion of lava boulders and redwood logs that they dubbed Wolf House. In August 1913—just days before they were to move in—a fire roared through the house, leaving only the stone shell. Devasted, the Londons never rebuilt. They lived instead in a modest cottage on the ranch, where Jack died at age 40. Trails lead past the ruins of **Wolf House**★ and the cottage where the man who penned such classic adventure stories as *The Call of the Wild*, *Sea Wolf* and *White Fang* lived and worked.

Petaluma Adobe State Historic Park★★

10mi west of Sonoma at 3325 Adobe Rd. Open year-round daily 10am–5pm. Closed Jan 1, Thanksgiving Day & Dec 25. $2. 707-762-4871. www.parks.ca.gov.

Mexican commander **Mariano Vallejo** chose this hilltop overlooking the rolling Sonoma County countryside as the site of his headquarters in 1834. Here he established a 100sq mi ranch on the land grant he received from the Mexican government. Rancho Petaluma thrived until Vallejo leased the property in September 1850. Today the restored two-story structure, half its initial size, re-creates the atmosphere of a prosperous ranch with authentic period pieces.

Don Clausen Fish Hatchery★★

3333 Skaggs Springs Rd. 11mi north of Healdsburg. Open daily 9:30am–4:30pm (closed Tue & Wed in winter). 707-433-9483. www.parks.sonoma.net./laktrls

Located behind the visitor center at **Lake Sonoma**★, this state-of-the-art hatchery building was created by the Army Corps of Engineers to lessen the environmental damage to Dry Creek when the dam was built. Here you can watch the spawning and hatching activities of steelhead trout, and coho and chinook salmon *(viewing times: Jan–Mar for steelhead trout; early Oct–Dec for salmon)*.

Lake Sonoma Overlook

11mi north of Healdsburg via Dry Creek Rd. Follow signs from Lake Sonoma visitor center. It's worth a drive up to this outlook for great **views**★★ of the hilly area surrounding the sapphire waters of **Lake Sonoma**★.

A Wine Country Sampler

There's seemingly no end to the wineries you can visit in Northern California's Wine Country, so we've provided a place to start. The following wineries were selected for the quality of visit (they combine wine production with fine art exhibits, innovative architecture and historical interest); their inclusion is not intended to be a comment on the wines. Complete lists of wineries and their hours are available from the visitors' bureaus in Napa Valley, Sonoma Valley and Russian River Valley *(see p 85)*. Most wineries offer tours and tastings *(most charge a tasting fee)*. Some offer tours by appointment only, so call before you go.

Beringer Vineyards★★ – *2000 Main St. (Hwy. 29), St. Helena. 707-963-7115. www.beringer.com.* The centerpiece of Napa Valley's oldest continuously operating winery, established in 1876 by German immigrants Jacob and Frederick Beringer, is the 17-room **Rhine House** (1883).

Buena Vista Winery★★ – *18000 Old Winery Rd., Sonoma. 707-938-1266. www.buenavistawinery.com.* Buena Vista was founded in 1857 by Hungarian immigrant Agoston Haraszthy, who was the first to experiment with European varietals in Northern California. The lovely stone **Press House** dates back to 1862.

Domaine Chandon★★ – *1 California Dr., Yountville. Take the Yountville Exit off Rte. 29 North. 707-944-2280. www.chandon.com.* The free guided tour of this winery, commissioned by the owners of France's famed Moët et Chandon, explains the principal stages of sparkling-wine production according to the traditional *méthode champenoise*. Splurge on California-French fare in the winery's **restaurant**.

Ferrari-Carano Winery★★ – *8761 Dry Creek Rd., 9mi north of Healdsburg. 707-433-6700. www.ferraricarano.com.* An Italian courtyard provides the formal entrance to the Renaissance-style **Villa Fiore** and its lovely **gardens**, which rise above the Dry Creek Valley.

Niebaum-Coppola Estate Winery★★ – *1991 St. Helena Hwy., Rutherford. 707-968-1100. www.niebaum-coppola.com.* The imposing 1882 stone winery here was built for Finnish sea captain Gustave Niebaum, who founded Inglenook Wines in 1879. Now owned by filmmaker Francis Ford Coppola, the winery houses the **Centennial Museum**, which explores both winemaking and film.

Sterling Vineyards★★ – *1111 Dunaweal Lane, Calistoga. Off Rte. 29, 1mi south of Calistoga. 707-942-3344. www.sterlingvineyards.com.* From the parking area, an **aerial tramway** transports you up to Sterling's winery, which perches atop a 300ft knoll overlooking the Napa Valley.

St. Supéry★★ – *8440 St. Helena Hwy./Rte. 29, Rutherford. 707-963-4507. www.stsupery.com.* Learn the ins and outs of the business of winemaking at St. Supéry's **Wine Discovery Center**★.

Benziger Family Winery★ – *1883 London Ranch Rd., Glen Ellen. 707-935-3000. www.benziger.com.* The tram tour of this sustainable winery takes visitors out into the vineyard to learn how the grapes are grown without using pesticides.

Berkeley★★

8mi northeast of San Francisco via I-80 over the Bay Bridge to Exit 11, and east on University Ave.; or take BART to Berkeley station. 510-549-7040 or 800-847-4823. www.visitberkeley.com.

A small city with a big reputation for political protest,
Berkeley offers much more
than a dynamic community.
A bustling university, a vast
collection of museums, and
excellent shopping and dining districts all add to the
city's appeal.

University of California, Berkeley★★

One block east (uphill) from the BART Berkeley Station.

UC Berkeley, which ranks among the
country's best universities in nearly all
of its academic programs, is notorious
for political activism and highly regarded for its scientific achievements.
Visit the campus to be inspired by the
proactive students and gorgeous architecture. Walking tours of the campus
depart from the **visitor center** *(101
University Hall; 510-642-5215;
www.berkeley.edu; Mon–Sat 10am, Sun
1pm)*. Along the way, you'll pass a
number of landmarks, including the
Valley Life Sciences Building★—the
largest academic building in the US
when it was completed in 1930. Climb
up to the observation platform in the

Scharffen Berger Factory Tour

*914 Heinz Ave. 510-981-4066.
www.scharffenberger.com.
Tours year-round daily at 10:30am,
2:30pm & 3:30pm.
Reservations recommended.*
Founded by longtime friends Robert
Steinberg and John Scharffenberger,
Scharffen Berger Chocolate Maker
specializes in small-batch process
pure dark chocolate. Learn how chocolate is made, from bean to bar, by
touring this acclaimed artisan shop-
and follow your nose to the retail
store to pick up some samples to go.

Campanile★★ (Sather Tower) for panoramic **views**★★ of the Berkeley Hills.
Depending on your interests, you may also want to visit the **UC Berkeley Art
Museum**★ *(2626 Bancroft Way; 510-642-0808; www.bampfa.berkeley.edu)* or
the **UC Botanical Garden**★ *(200 Centennial Dr.; 510-643-2755; http://botanic
algarden.berkeley.edu)*.

Telegraph Avenue★

Between Bancroft & Dwight Ways.

A haven for the intellectually elite and the chronically hip, this little street is
packed with bookstores, museums, art vendors, brew pubs, record stores and
cafes. Stop by and soak up the culture.

Carmel★★

120mi south of San Francisco via US-101 South to Rte. 156 West to Hwy. 1 South. Tourist information: 831-624-2522 or www.carmelcalifornia.org.

Many visitors to San Francisco plan extra time for a sojourn south to tony Carmel-by-the-Sea, as it's officially named. Arcing along the coastline just below the point of the Monterey Peninsula, Carmel covers a charming square mile of gorgeous wide **beach★★** and carefully tended cottages.

Carmel's quaint village ambience is protected by a strict 1929 zoning ordinance that outlaws sidewalks, street lights and mailboxes in residential areas. However, you'll find upscale boutiques, galleries, inns and restaurants galore in the commercial area *(Ocean, 6th & 7th Aves. between Junipero Ave. & Monte Verde St.)*. Keep your eye out for famous resident Clint Eastwood, who was Carmel's mayor in the mid-1980s.

San Carlos Borroméo de Carmelo Mission★★★

3080 Rio Rd. at Lasuen Dr. 831-624-3600. www.carmelmission.org. Open year-round Mon—Fri 9:30am—4:30pm, weekends 10:30am—4:30pm. Closed Thanksgiving Day & Dec 25. $4.

A Perch for Poets

Quiet Carmel developed a reputation as a bohemian retreat in the early 20C, when poets like **Robinson Jeffers** came to town. In 1918 Jeffers built a small stone complex on the tor, or rock promontory, overlooking the bay on Carmel Point. Today you can tour **Tor House★★**, where Jeffers died in 1962 at age 75 *(26304 Ocean View Ave.; 831-624-1813; www.torhouse.org; visit by guided tour only, reservations required; Fri & Sat 10am—3pm; $7; children under 12 not allowed).*

Headquarters of the California mission chain during its expansive early years, the Carmel mission reflects the visionary spirit of its founder, **Padre Junípero Serra**, who moved the mission here from the presidio at Monterey in 1771. The striking 1797 sandstone **church** and rebuilt mission grounds, named in honor of the canonized 16C cardinal St. Charles (Carlos) Borromeo, continue to serve as an active parish church and school.

In the reconstructed adobe **Padres' Quarters** you'll find Serra's cell, where the weary padre died at age 71. His remains lie under the church sanctuary.

Point Lobos State Reserve★★

Off Hwy. 1, 3.5mi south of Carmel. Open Apr—Sept daily 9am—7pm. Rest of the year daily 9am—5pm. $2. 831-624-4909. www.parks.ca.gov.

Take time for a walk at this spectacular 1,250-acre park at the southern end of Carmel Bay, where trails lead around the headlands past aquamarine **China Cove★** and the gnarled forms of rare Monterey Cypress trees. Be sure to check out **Sea Lion Point** on the peninsula's rocky edge, named for the noisy pinnipeds that hang out there.

Marin Headlands★★

3mi north of San Francisco. Take US-101 north across the Golden Gate Bridge (toll $5 southbound only) to the Alexander Ave. exit and follow the signs. Visitor center: 415-331-1540. www.nps.gov/goga/mahe.

With jaw-dropping views of the Golden Gate Bridge, the Pacific Ocean and San Francisco Bay, the Marin Headlands attract throngs of visitors each year. A member of the GGNRA *(see Parks and Gardens)* since 1972, the site was previously controlled by the US Army.

Conzelman Road★★★

Take US-101 north across the Golden Gate Bride to the exit for Alexander Ave. Pass under the freeway and continue to Conzelman Rd.

One of the best ways to tour the headlands is to follow this scenic route that winds past abandoned military batteries. The road offers plenty of turnouts so you can appreciate the outstanding **views★★★**.

Mount Tamalpais State Park★★

801 Panoramic Hwy., Mill Valley. Take US-101 North to Hwy. 1; exit at Stinson Beach and follow signs. 415-388-2070. www.parks.ca.gov. Open daily 7am–sunset. $4.

People began visiting Mt. Tamalpais during the Gold Rush years, and shortly thereafter, hiking trails and transportation lines were added to accommodate tourists. By 1896, visitors could ride the Mt. Tamalpais Scenic Railway, known as "the Crookedest Railway in the World." Although the railroad was destroyed in 1930, the mountain still has plenty to offer. With over 50mi of trails, the park is a haven for hikers and mountain bikers. If sitting back and enjoying the scenery is more your style, head to **East Peak**, which offers some of the best **views★★★** in the Bay Area.

Fun for Kids: Bay Area Discovery Museum★

At the Discovery Museum, kids get an awesome introduction to art, science and the environment through hands-on exhibits *(557 McReynolds Rd., East Fort Baker; 415-339-3900; www.baykidsmuseum.org; open Tue–Fri 9am–4pm, weekends 10am–5pm; $7 adults & children)*. After your visit, check out **Fort Baker**, the first military post on the north side of the Golden Gate, and walk along the bluffs overlooking Horseshoe Cove for **views★★** of the Golden Gate Bridge. *To get to the museum or Fort Baker, head north over the Golden Gate Bridge and take the Alexander Ave. exit; then turn left onto Bunker Rd. and follow signs.*

Mendocino★★

150mi north of San Francisco via US-101 north to Rte. 128 west, or follow scenic Hwy. 1 north along the coast. Visitor information: 866-466-3636; www.gomendo.com or www.mendocino.com.

Less than half a day's drive north of San Francisco brings you to this picture-perfect village, set high on a rocky headland where the Big River meets the ocean. You may well think you're in a New England seaside village when you see Mendocino's **Main Street★**, a quaint strip of pastel-painted Victorian clapboard buildings. There's a reason for that: Mendocino's founders hailed from the northeast and copied, as nearly as they could, the design of the homes they had left behind.

Named for Antonio de Mendoza, the first viceroy of New Spain, Mendocino got its start as a lumber town in the mid-19C. The majority of the present-day architecture was constructed after 1870, the year a fire destroyed most of the town's original buildings. Wooden water towers, powered by windmills more than 100 years ago, still store precious water that is pumped from the town's wells.

Today Mendocino caters to tourists, who come here to spend a few peaceful days in charming B&Bs, shop in artisans' boutiques and fine-arts galleries, and revel in stunning views of the turquoise waters of Mendocino Bay.

Mendocino in the Movies

Over the years, Hollywood directors have also favored the town's quaint ambience, using its quiet streets as the settings for a number of productions, including the films *Johnny Belinda* (1947) and *The Russians Are Coming, The Russians Are Coming* (1966). You may recognize the house at 45110 Little Lake Street as the Cabot Cove, Maine, home of Jessica Fletcher, from the TV series *Murder, She Wrote* (1984–1996).

Mendocino Headlands State Park★★

707-937-5804. www.parks.ca.gov. Open year-round daily dawn–dusk.

Enveloping the town on three sides, these pristine headlands are laced by paths that reveal spectacular **views★★** of the Mendocino coast with its fissure-riddled rocks and sea caves. This is a great place to watch for migrating whales *(southbound Nov–Dec, northbound Feb–Mar)*, and in spring, the multicolored wildflowers are astounding. The 1854 **Ford House Museum** serves as the park's visitor center *(735 Main St.; 707-937-5397; open year-round daily 11am–4pm)*.

Best Excursions From San Francisco

Monterey★★

115mi south of San Francisco. Follow US-101 south to Rte. 156 west to Hwy. 1 South. Visitor information: 831-649-1770 or 888-221-1010; www.montereyinfo.org.

Once capital of California and later of sardines, Monterey mixes its Spanish colonial past with modern appeal. Bookworms come here to pay homage to John Steinbeck at **Cannery Row★** and to Robert Louis Stevenson at the **Stevenson House★** *(530 Houston St.; 831-649-7118)*. Even if literature doesn't appeal to you, the city is a delight, featuring a world-class aquarium, a large collection of historical sites, and fabulous shops.

Path of History Walking Tour — This tour is a great way to visit Monterey's historic sites. **Monterey State Historic Park** *(831-649-7118; www.parks.ca.gov)* maintains many of the adobes along the route and offers guided walking tours throughout the year.

Monterey Bay Aquarium★★

886 Cannery Row. 831-648-4888. www.mbayaq.org. Open Jun–Aug daily 9:30am–6pm. Rest of the year daily 10am–6pm. Closed Dec 25. $19.95.

If you're wondering what denizens lurk beneath the waters of Monterey Bay, you've come to the right place—more than 250,000 animals and plants representing 550 species swim and sway here. Housed in a converted cannery, the aquarium is designed to incorporate the sea as an architectural element. You'll understand how when you look through the 56ft-long window into **The Outer Bay★★**, an open-ocean tank that holds a million gallons of seawater. Whether you go alone to learn the truth about *Jaws* in the new shark exhibit or take the kids to the hands-on **Splash Zone★**, you're sure to enjoy this award-winning aquarium.

17-Mile Drive★★

Access via Pacific Grove Gate, off Sunset Dr.; Country Club Gate, off Congress Ave.; Samuel B. Morse Gate, off Rte. 68; Hwy. 1 Gate; and Carmel Gate, off San Antonio Blvd. $8.50/car.
When the elegant Del Monte Hotel opened in 1880, it put Monterey on the map. Guests here loved taking horse-drawn carriage rides along the gravel trail skirting Monterey Peninsula. Today you can drive your car on the private 17-Mile Drive toll road. Along the way, you'll revel in exquisite **views★★★** of the Pacific Ocean, groves of gnarled Monterey cypress trees, and the luxuriant oceanside course of the famed Pebble Beach Golf Links. Don't miss the **Lone Cypress**, which has clung stubbornly to its bald rock promontory for more than 200 years.

Point Reyes National Seashore★★

40mi north of San Francisco. Take US-101 north to the Greenbrae exit and follow Sir Francis Drake Blvd. west for 10mi; then take Hwy. 1 to Bear Valley Rd. 415-464-5100. www.nps.gov/pore. Open year-round daily dawn–dusk.

This foggy wind-whipped stretch of coast is as treacherous as it is beautiful. Indeed, many a ship has met its demise over the years along the rocky shores of Point Reyes peninsula. Today the coastline here is a national seashore (so-designated in 1962), harboring a vast assortment of animals, along with serene beaches and splendid views (on clear days). Don't forget your camera.

Point Reyes Lighthouse★★

End of Sir Francis Drake Blvd. Visitor center & lighthouse open year-round Thu–Mon 10am–4:30pm.

With a three-ton Fresnel lens visible for 24 nautical miles, the Point Reyes Lighthouse saved countless lives as it routed ships safely around the rocky shores of Point Reyes. You can still view the lens today—if you're willing to brave the 308 steps leading down to the light. On clear days, the lighthouse offers spectacular **views**★★★

of the coast, the offshore Farallon Islands and San Francisco. If you're here between December and April, bring binoculars to watch gray whales pass near the shore during their annual migration. Sea lions and seals congregate just east of the point, and Chimney Rock is one of the best places to see elephant seals in the Bay Area.

Tips for Visiting

Stop by the **Bear Valley Visitor Center**★ *(open year-round Mon–Fri 9am–5pm, weekends 8am–5pm)* to gather information and brush up on your knowledge of the area. From here, you can take the kids for a walk along **Earthquake Trail**★ *(.6mi)*, where you'll see the dramatic ground-shifting of the 1906 quake, or on the **Woodpecker Nature Trail** *(.7mi)*, to discover natural wonders. Additional information centers are located at Drakes Beach and Point Reyes Lighthouse.

Bear Valley Trail★

8.2mi round-trip. Trailhead near visitor center.

This wide, easy-to-navigate path follows Coast Creek to the Arch Rock **viewpoint** overlooking the ocean. Mingle with hikers, bikers and runners as you pass through redwood forests and the picnic-perfect Divide Meadow. Need more of a challenge? Try the Sky, Glen or Old Pine trails; all three branch off the Bear Valley path.

Sonoma County Coast★★

Along Hwy. 1 from Point Reyes Station north to Mendocino County. Visitor's information: 850 Hwy. 1, in Bodega Bay. 707-875-3866. www.BodegaBay.com.

Sites described below are organized from south to north.

Stretching 191mi from San Francisco to north of Fort Bragg, Highway 1 snakes along the rim of the southern half of California's North Coast. Over the centuries, the Pacific's waves have carved the shale and sandstone Franciscan rocks of the coastline here into vertical benches backed by craggy cliffs. It's worth a drive up at least as far north as Mendocino *(see p 97)* for spectacular **views** of steep, rocky walls being pummeled by the roiling Pacific surf.

Sonoma Coast State Beaches★★

707-875-3483. www.parks.ca.gov. Open daily year-round. $4/vehicle.

Rocky outcrops separate the 15 small, sandy crescents that punctuate this 16mi strip of coast from Bodega Head *(65mi north of San Francisco)* to just north of Jenner. Stop at the abundant turnouts along this part of Highway 1 to ogle spectacular oceanscapes, or just spend some time sunbathing or picnicking at the beaches. One of the most accessible of the Sonoma Coast beaches is **Goat Rock Beach**★ at the mouth of the Russian River, where you'll have a unique view of river and ocean barely separated by a narrow spit of sand. From November to March, throngs of resident harbor seals vie with fishermen here to catch the schools of salmon that return each year to spawn. North of Jenner, it's slow going as the road becomes a series of sharply angled switchbacks winding high above the ocean.

Fort Ross State Historic Park★★

87mi north of San Francisco on Hwy. 1. 707-847-3286. www.parks.ca.gov. Grounds open year-round daily dawn–dusk. Visitor center open year-round daily 10am–4:30pm. Closed Thanksgiving Day & Dec 25. $4/vehicle.

You probably wouldn't expect to see a Russian fort on the coast of California. Settlement Rossiia (Russia) was established in 1812 by members of the Russian-American Company, a commercial hunting and trading group authorized by the tsarist government to manage Russian trade and exploration in North America. Built high on an isolated promontory above a sheltered azure cove,

Fort Ross reigned as Russia's easternmost outpost for nearly 40 years.

The redwood fort, now owned by the State of California, has been partially restored. Modeled after traditional edifices in Siberia, the stockade contains six structures, including the partially original **Rotchev House**.

East Bay Area★

East of San Francisco. Take I-80 East across the San Francisco-Oakland Bay Bridge.

Nestled among the small towns that extend east of Oakland and Berkeley lie a number of lesser-known, though equally significant, must-sees.

Blackhawk Museum★★

3700 Blackhawk Plaza Circle, Danville. 33mi east of San Francisco. via I-680 to Sycamore Valley Blvd. exit. 925-736-2277. www.blackhawkauto.org. Open Wed–Sat 10am–5pm. $8.

With more than 90 vintage automobiles on display dating from the 1890s to the 1960s, this museum will appeal to anyone who loves the feel of the open road.

Eugene O'Neill National Historic Site★★

Kuss Rd., Danville. 28mi east of San Francisco. Take I-80 East to Hwy 24; drive east on Hwy. 24 to I-680, and take I-680 south from Walnut Creek to Danville. 925-838-0249. www.nps.gov/euon. Open Mon–Fri 8am–4:30pm. Closed Jan 1, Thanksgiving Day & Dec 25. Reservations required.

The Skinny on Eugene O'Neill

- Eugene Gladstone O'Neill (1888–1953) won Pulitzer Prizes for three of his dramas: *Anna Christie*, *Strange Interlude*, and *Long Day's Journey Into Night*.
- O'Neill is the only American playwright to win the Nobel Prize for Literature (in 1936).

If you love theater and literature, be sure to tour this site, home of Tau House, where playwright Eugene O'Neill lived and worked from 1937 to 1944. The famous playwright wrote his best-known works here, including *The Iceman Cometh* and the autobiographical *A Long Day's Journey into Night*.

John Muir National Historic Site★

4202 Alhambra Ave., Martinez. 30mi northeast of San Francisco. 925-228-8860. www.nps.gov/jomu. Follow I-80 East to Exit 24 and take Rte. 4 east; exit at Alhambra Ave. and turn left. Open year-round Wed–Sun 10am–5pm. Closed Jan 1, Thanksgiving Day & Dec 25. $3.

Often called "The Father of our National Park System," John Muir *(see p 84)* was one of America's first conservationists. Muir spent the last years of his life, from 1890 until his death in 1914, at this two-story Italianate home.

Mount Diablo State Park★

North Gate Rd., Walnut Creek. 35mi east of San Francisco. From Oakland, take Rte. 24 East to Walnut Creek and go east on Ygnacio Valley Rd.; turn right on Walnut Ave. 925-837-2525. www.mdia.org. Open daily 8am–dusk. $4/car.

Ready for a hike? If you make it to the top of 3,849ft-high Mount Diablo here, you'll be rewarded with an extensive breathtaking view★★★ that stretches as far as Mount Lassen (165mi northeast).

Oakland★

12mi east of San Francisco. Take I-80 across the San Francisco-Oakland Bay Bridge. Tourist information: 510-839-9000 or www.oaklandcvb.com.

Just a short hop across the Bay Bridge from San Francisco, Oakland makes a great excursion for anyone in the Bay Area who wants to give his wallet a break from the high costs of the city. Kids, sports fans, and shopaholics will all find something to occupy them in this city across the Bay.

Oakland Museum of California★★

1000 Oak St. 510-238-2200. www.museumca.org. Open Wed–Sat 10am–5pm, Sun noon–5pm, (open until 9pm the 2nd Fri of every month). Closed major holidays. $8.

Designed to explain and promote California, the Oakland Museum will introduce you to the art, history, and natural sciences unique to California. The 7.7-acre cultural complex celebrates California's diversity on all three floors of the building that *New York Times* critic Ada Louise Huxtable deemed "one of the most thoughtful revolutionary structures in the world."

Paramount Theatre★★

2025 Broadway St. 510-465-6400. www.paramounttheatre.org.

A striking example of Art Deco architecture, the Paramount Theatre currently serves as both a movie theater and a performing-arts center. Drop by to see either the Oakland Ballet or the Oakland East Bay Symphony perform, or, if you're a history buff, take a tour of the complex.

USS Hornet★★

Pier 3, Alameda. Take Atlantic Ave. north off Webster St. (Rte. 61) and follow signs. 510-521-8448. www.uss-hornet.org. Open year-round Wed–Mon 10am–5pm, Tue 10am–3pm. Closed Jan 1, Thanksgiving Day & Dec 25. $12.

Be sure to explore the USS *Hornet*, one of the most distinguished military ships in US history. Commissioned in 1943, this aircraft carrier served 16 consecutive months in the Pacific Campaign during World War II. After earning nine battle stars for its service in that war, the *Hornet* went on to serve in Vietnam and later to recover the astronauts of Apollo 11.

Jack London Square★

Along the Embarcadero from Clay to Alice Sts. 510-814-6000. www.jacklondonsquare.com.

If you want to shop, dine, or enjoy the scenery, head to this once-gritty dock area. Named for the writer who lived in Oakland in his early years, Jack London Square boasts a plethora of stores and restaurants as well as a hip nightlife scene.

Sausalito ★

3mi north of San Francisco. Take US-101 over the Golden Gate Bridge to the Alexander Ave. exit and continue 2mi to Bridgeway Blvd. Visitor information: 415-331-1093 or www.sausalito.org.

Need a short break from the city? Hop a ferry from San Francisco to this sophisticated waterfront community. Not only is Sausalito an excellent launching point for visits to the Marin Headlands and the Wine Country, but with its upscale boutiques, gorgeous views and charming ambience, Sausalito is also a wonderful place to relax and recharge.

For ferry information, contact the Blue and Gold Fleet (415-705-5555; www.blueandgoldfleet.com; $7.25 one way), or Golden Gate Ferry (415-923-2000; www.goldengateferry.com; $5.60 one way). Call or check Web sites for schedules.

Bridgeway Boulevard ★

Attention shoppers: Make a beeline for Sausalito's commercial district, which parallels the Sausalito waterfront. Originally called Water Street, Bridgeway is the district's main drag. Here, you can shop 'til you drop and then sit back in a cafe to admire the **views**★★ of the city and bay—**Horizons**, at 558 Bridgeway, boasts a great deck right on the water. Stop for information at the **Sausalito Visitor Center & Historical Exhibit** *(780 Bridgeway; open year-round Tue–Sun 11:30am–4pm; 415-332-0505)*. Housed in a former ice house, the center features photographic displays of the Golden Gate Bridge.

Bay Model Visitor's Center ★ – *2100 Bridgeway. 415-332-3870. www.spn.usace.army.mil/bmvc.* Learn about the environment on the self-guided tour of this 1.5-acre scale model of the San Francisco Bay and Sacramento-San Joaquin Delta, originally built by the US Army Corps of Engineers to test the effect of dams on the Bay.

Sausalito Shopping

Here's a sampling of the shops and galleries unique to Sausalito:

Art That Makes You Laugh – *607 Bridgeway. 415-331-1755. www.leedyart.com.* Jeff Leedy's off-center art gallery features originals and reproductions.

Fingerhut Gallery – *690 Bridgeway. 415-331-7225. www.fingerhutart.com.* Here you'll find fine art (read pricey!) by the likes of masters Chagall, Matisse and Picasso.

Gene Hiller for Men – *729 Bridgeway. 415-332-3636. www.genehiller.com.* One of California's premier men's clothiers proffers designs by Brioni and Canali, among other notables.

Petri's Gallery – *675 Bridgeway. 415-332-2225. www.petrisgallery.com.* Petri's carries art glass from over 150 designers.

The venues listed below were selected for their ambience, location and/or value for money. Rates indicate the average cost of an appetizer, an entrée and a dessert for one person (not including tax, gratuity or beverages). Most restaurants are open daily and accept major credit cards. Call for information regarding reservations, dress code and opening hours. Restaurants listed are located in San Francisco unless otherwise noted. For a complete listing of restaurants mentioned in this guide, see Index.

$$$$ over $50   **$$ $15–$30**
$$$ $30–$50   **$ less than $15**

Luxury

Aqua $$$$ Seafood

252 California St., Financial District. 415-956-9662. www.aqua-sf.com.

Oversize mirrors and looming floral displays add a sense of elegance to this soothing space with its salmon-colored walls and muted tones. Ahi tuna here is spice-encrusted and served with artisan foie gras; King salmon is steamed "en papillote," napped with warm dill and caviar cream and served with lemon-potato croquettes. Two different six-course tasting menus are available nightly for $95. Aqua's $29 two-course business lunch draws movers and shakers from the expense-account set.

Boulevard $$$$ New American

1 Mission St., Embarcadero. 415-543-6084. www.boulevardrestaurant.com.

Belle Epoque accents—mosaic tile, steel girders, a pressed-tin ceiling—have transformed the 1889 Audiffred Building, whose windows frame the Bay Bridge. Chef Nancy Oakes melds Asian and Mediterranean elements with classic French techniques in dishes like pan-roasted Maine cod fish and lobster tart, and wood-oven-roasted lamb sirloin stuffed with artichokes, tiny Italian olives and parsley. For dessert, the decadent chocolate tasting (five chocolate treats, including a chocolate truffle tart and mocha pot de crème) will satisfy the most ardent chocoholic.

Chez Panisse $$$$ California

1517 Shattuck Ave., Berkeley. Dinner only. Closed Sun. 510-548-5525. www.chezpanisse.com.

California cuisine was born in 1971 in this casual dining room, under the watchful eye of culinary doyenne Alice Waters. It's well worth the drive over to Berkeley to sample stellar four-course prix-fixe menus change nightly (make reservations a month in advance); Provençal fish stew cooked in the fireplace, spit-roasted Niman Ranch pork tenderloin with herb-spice crust and Zinfandel sauce, and Meyer lemon Shaker tart are just a taste of what you might find on the menu. Upstairs, the boisterous **Chez Panisse Café ($$$)** serves simpler fare for lunch and dinner.

Farallon $$$$ Seafood

450 Post St., Union Square. 415-956-6969. www.farallonrestaurant.com.

Whimsical blown-glass jellyfish chandeliers float over tables, octopus stools nestle beside kelp columns— these and other flamboyant undersea fantasies complement chef Mark Franz's seafood menu here. Wash down entrées—sautéed North Atlantic skate wing with morel mushroom sauce; grilled line-caught Pacific ono with grilled clams and saffron butter— with a selection from the extensive wine list.

Fifth Floor $$$$ New French

12 Fourth St., in the Hotel Palomar, Yerba Buena Gardens. Dinner only. Closed Sun. 415-348-1555. www.fifthfloor.citysearch.com.

Subtle lighting plays across red leather and velvet banquettes in the Hotel Palomar's clubby dining room, where dark polished woods are set off against a zebra-striped carpet. Now presided over by chef Laurent Gras, whose credits include work at three Michelin-starred restaurants in France, the kitchen turns out innovative seasonal fare like Colorado lamb loin baked with linden leaves and forest mushrooms. Aside from the à la carte selections, a chef's tasting menu *($95)* and a pre-theater tasting menu *($65)* are offered nightly.

Fleur de Lys $$$$ New French

777 Sutter St., Union Square. Closed Sun. 415-673-7779. www.fleurdelyssf.com.

French-born chef and owner Hubert Keller adds California flair to his three tasting menus *(3 courses, $65; 4 courses, $72; 5 courses, $80)* at Fleur de Lys. Roasted squab breasts filled with foie gras, peppered filet mignon on braised endive, and monkfish rolled in aged Serrano ham represent a sampling of Keller's artistry. For non-meat eaters, a vegetarian tasting menu is always an option. Renovated following a 2001 fire, the main dining room is tented with 900 yards of custom-printed fabric.

Gary Danko $$$$ Continental

800 North Point St. at Hyde St., Fisherman's Wharf. Dinner only. 415-749-2060. www.garydanko.com.

Elegant but understated decor—plantation shutters and soothing earth tones—allows chef-owner Danko's culinary creations to take center stage. Three-, four- or five-course tasting menus (ranging in price from $58 to $78) can be paired with wines (for an additional charge) and include traditional Asian-style tea service. Choices reflect seasonal ingredients such as seared foie gras with carmelized red onions and quince and pomegranate seeds, pan-fried Branzino bass with braised fennel and picholine olives, and roasted pears and gingerbread with pumpkin ice cream.

Jardinière $$$$ California-French

300 Grove St. at Franklin St., Civic Center. Dinner only. 415-861-5555. www.jardiniere.com.

Hundreds of bubbles sparkle on the domed ceiling of the Champagne Rotunda in this sophisticated restaurant, favored for pre- or post-theater dining. Chef and co-owner Traci Des Jardins may treat diners to Maine diver scallops with potato purée and black-truffle nage or Liberty Farms duck breast with creamed nettles; you never know exactly what awaits you, as the menu changes daily.

Masa's $$$$ French

648 Bush St., in the Executive Hotel Vintage Court, Union Square. 415-989-7154. www.vintagecourt.com.

A redo in 2001 transformed this dining room into a sleek space bathed in warm brown tones with chocolate mohair banquettes, toile-covered chairs and red silk Chinese lanterns. Diners can choose from daily tasting menus of three *($65),* six *($85)* or nine *($115)* courses. Your meal here might start with lobster consommé, progress to milk-fed *poularde* with Italian butter beans and artichokes, and end with rum and lime bananas accompanied by coconut-milk ice cream.

Moderate

Cortez $$$ Mediterranean

550 Geary St., in the Hotel Adagio, Union Square. Dinner only. 415-292-6360.
www.cortezrestaurant.com.

Mulitcolored orb light fixtures seem to float above
this boisterous dining room across from the Geary
Theater. But there's more that's hip here than the
decor. Small plates such as roasted branzino with
oven-dried tomatoes and caper brown butter, and
date-and-mint-crusted Niman Ranch rack of lamb
satisfy both big and small appetites (how much you
spend depends on how many you order). Save room for dessert—each selection,
from sugar-and-spice beignets with Valhrona chocolate fondue to lemon me-
ringue tart with ginger ice cream, is paired with a dessert wine or liqueur.

Delfina $$$ Italian

3621 18th St., Mission District. 415-552-4055.

One of the hottest tables in town, this neighborhood
gem is operated by husband-and-wife team Craig Stoll
and Anne Spencer. Simple food and stellar service rule in
the long, narrow dining room, where chef Stoll creates
comfort-food masterpieces out of the freshest seasonal
ingredients from San Francisco's farmers' markets. House-made pastas may be
sauced with succulent mussels, and roasted lamb shank is braised in wine. If it's
on the nightly changing menu, order the silky panna cotta for dessert.

Empress of China $$$ Chinese

838 Grant Ave., Chinatown. 415-434-1345. www.empressofchinasf.citysearch.com.

The focal point of this sixth-floor restaurant is a central pagoda whose 30ft-
diameter octagonal wooden pavilion was built by craftsmen in Taiwan and
reassembled here. You'll feast on regional Chinese dishes—Mongolian beef,
Peking duck, Mongolian hundred-blossom lamb, lobster Cantonese—while
enjoying the views through windows that overlook the bustling Chinatown
street scene.

Fog City Diner $$$ American

1300 Battery St., Embarcadero. 415-982-2000. www.fogcitydiner.com.

You'll recognize this chrome and neon landmark at the foot of Telegraph Hill by
the clock over its door, which advises patrons: "Don't Worry." Inside you'll find

1930s roadside-diner ambience as well as upscale
burgers with "Phenomenal French fries," Dungeness
crab cioppino, "mighty" meatloaf with wild mush
room gravy, and a crispy reddened snapper sandwich.
Diners on a budget often opt for the eclectic small
plates: Point Reyes blue cheese fritters, mu shu pork
burritos, tuna avocado tartar.

Greens $$$ Vegetarian

Fort Mason Center, Bldg. A, Marina District. 415-771-6222. www.greensrest.citysearch.com.

Opened in 1979 by disciples of the San Francisco Zen Center, this gourmet veggie restaurant west of Fisherman's Wharf gets much of its organic produce from the center's Green Gulch Farm in Marin County. Reserve ahead for lunch or dinner, and savor such seasonal fare as fresh pea ravioli with saffron butter, grilled fennel pizza or maybe a filo strata of artichokes, crimini mushrooms, leeks, walnuts and ricotta, along with wonderful views of the marina with the Golden Gate Bridge in the distance. The wine list here has won national awards.

John's Grill $$$ American

63 Ellis St., Union Square. 415-986-0069. www.johnsgrill.com.

The true Maltese Falcon, made famous by author and former patron Dashiell Hammet (and actor Humphrey Bogart), has been at home behind the bar here since 1908. The grill's dark, moody interior is straight out of film noir. Signature dishes chicken Jerusalem (chicken sautéed with artichokes and mushroom in a white-wine-cream sauce) and oysters Wellington (baked in puff pastry with creamed spinach and smoky bacon) share menu space with a host of steaks and seafood.

McCormick & Kuleto's $$$ Seafood

900 North Point St., Fisherman's Wharf. 415-929-1730. www.mccormickandkuletos.com.

Some of the best seafood in the wharf area is served not on the water but at this spacious and lively restaurant in Ghirardelli Square. Tables on two levels boast great bay views toward Alcatraz. In the bar area, clubby wood and Art Deco appointments prevail. There's a full oyster bar and a long list of fresh fish and shellfish, from Petrale sole and Ahi tuna to Dungeness crab and wild Columbia River sturgeon, all cooked to order. Sunday brunch (served until 3pm) includes Hangtown Fry, a scrambled-egg dish with fried yearling oysters.

Moose's $$$ New American

1652 Stockton St., North Beach. 415-989-7800. www.mooses.com.

For four decades, owner Ed Moose has lured a legion of actors and athletes, politicos and business people, and local society types to his boisterous bar and grill on Washington Square. Depending on the season, the menu may offer the likes of bluenose bass, wild Alaskan halibut, pumpkin ravioli, and braised lamb shank—but the time-honored Mooseburger is always available. Desserts include an ice-cream sandwich updated with bittersweet chocolate ice cream and chambord-and-white-chocolate dipping sauce. Diners enjoy live jazz nightly from 8pm to 11pm.

Restaurant LuLu $$$ Mediterranean

816 Folsom St., SoMa. 415-495-5775. www.lulu.citysearch.com.

Occupying a beautifully renovated warehouse a block from the Moscone Convention Center, LuLu's open kitchen focuses on wood-fired pizzas and rotisserie-grilled meats. Nightly rotisserie specials range from farm-raised squab to suckling pig. Save room for profiteroles with coffee ice cream and warm Valrhona chocolate sauce. LuLu's little sister, a gourmet deli called Petite LuLu, recently opened in the remodeled Ferry Building *(see Landmarks)*.

Rose Pistola $$$ Italian

532 Columbus Ave., North Beach. 415-399-0499.

A wood-burning oven dominates the open kitchen in this bustling eatery, which won the James Beard Best New Restaurant award in 1997. The menu here echoes traditional Ligurian fare prepared by the Italian immigrants who settled in North Beach in the city's early days. Local fish and shellfish star in such dishes as cioppino (San Francisco's answer to bouillabaise) and whole striped bass with fennel, potato and tapenade—many of which are served family-style on large platters. In good weather, enjoy people-watching from the sidewalk tables.

The Slanted Door $$$ Vietnamese

1 Ferry Building, Embarcadero. 415-861-8032. www.slanteddoor.com.

Recently relocated to its new digs in the renovated Ferry Building, the Slanted Door offers wonderful Vietnamese-inspired cuisine. Crowds arrive early for grapefruit and jicama salad; spring rolls stuffed with pork, shrimp and mint; fresh Dungeness crab with cellophane noodles; and crispy five-spice Liberty duck leg. Parties of eight or more can order a combination of dishes to share from the prix-fixe menu *($35/person)*.

Zuni Café $$$ Mediterranean

1658 Market St., Civic Center. Closed Mon. 415-552-2522.

Opened some 20 years ago by chef Judy Rodgers as a southwestern restaurant (thus the name), Zuni now offers hearty southern French and Italian food infused with California flavors. Classics on the ever-changing menu include the succulent brick-oven-roasted chicken and the signature Caesar salad. An eclectic clientele crowd around the copper oyster-and-champagne bar.

Budget

Betelnut Pejiu Wu $$ Asian-Fusion

2030 Union St., Cow Hollow. 415-929-8855. www.betelnutrestaurant.com.

Fashioned after a traditional Southeast Asian *pejiu wu*, or beer house, Betelnut serves fresh regional "street food" in a British Colonial atmosphere with overhead fans swirling beside sensuous paintings of Asian women. Popular small plates and signature dishes like galanga beef (filet mignon marinated in galanga powder, sesame oil, oyster sauce and Xoashing rice wok-seared with garlic and red and green Thai chilis) tend to be spicy—all the better to wash them down with a large mug of imported beer.

Café de la Presse $$ French

469 Bush St., Chinatown. 415-249-0900. www.cafedelapresse.com.

Casual brasserie meals are served at this cafe and international newsstand beside Chinatown Gate. The menu features French onion soup topped with cheese, crab-and-mushroom cassolette with Mornay sauce, and grilled tournedos of beef with sautéed "Parisian" potatoes. A favorite of foreign residents and visitors is the espresso bar, with its tempting selection of pastries.

Chez Nous $$ Mediterranean

1911 Fillmore St., Pacific Heights. 415-441-8044.

Now that they take reservations, you don't have to wait for a table at this small, but always crowded, tapas restaurant. Settle in at the bar for a glass of wine and some warm olives and crusty bread while you wait. Melt-in-your-mouth lamb chops with lavender sea salt, grilled squid tossed with olives, fennel and greens, and Mediterranean fish soup will keep you coming back for more.

Fior d'Italia $$ Northern Italian

601 Union St., North Beach 415-986-1886. www.fior.com.

America's oldest Italian restaurant, this institution opened in 1886 and has faced Washington Square since 1954. Historical photos line the walls; the Tony Bennett Room honors San Francisco's favorite crooner. The extensive menu offers traditional Northern Italian fare, from minestrone and house-made pasta to beef, veal and seafood to risotto and polenta. Fior's calamari, gnocchi, osso buco and Caesar salad are consistently hailed as some of the best in the city.

The Stinking Rose $$ California-Italian

325 Columbus Ave., North Beach. 415-781-7673. www.thestinkingrose.com.

Not a place to take that first date, the Stinking Rose specializes in food redolent with garlic—lots and lots of garlic.
Start with the bagna calda, garlic roasted in olive oil and
butter presented in a hot skillet with bread for dipping.
Forty-clove garlic chicken is roasted on the bone and served
with—what else?—garlic mashed potatoes. If you really feel
adventurous, try garlic ice cream for dessert. The menu
notes that "Vampire Fare" can be prepared without garlic.

Swan Oyster Depot $$ Seafood

1517 Polk St., Nob Hill. Open 8am–5:30pm. Closed Sun. 415-673-1101.

The Sancimino family has operated this tiny fish market and eatery since 1946.
In the window, the day's catch stops passers-by; inside, jokes fly as shells are
shucked. Take a seat at the marble counter—it's your only option, there are no
tables—and order a bowl of buttery clam chowder, a plate of cracked Dungeness crab or a platter of oysters and clams on the half-shell. Wash it down
with a cold glass of San Francisco's Anchor Steam bear and you'll leave a happy
camper. Don't bother bringing your credit cards; Swan's only accepts cash.

Thirsty Bear Brewing Company $$ Spanish

661 Howard St., Yerba Buena Gardens. 415-974-0905. www.thirstybear.com.

At Thirsty Bear, dozens of cold and hot tapas plates complement nine different house-made brews on tap, which range from Polar Bear Ale, a lightly
hopped pilsner, to Meyer E.S.B., an extra special bitter. Nosh on fish cheeks
with sherry-garlic sauce, crispy chickpea cakes, and grilled-lamb "lollipop," or
try one of three different versions of paella—seafood, vegetarian, and Valen-
ciana, a mix of meat, seafood and vegetables on saffron rice.

Yank Sing $$ Chinese

*49 Stevenson St. and One Rincon Center (101 Spear St.), SoMa. Lunch only. 415-957-9300.
www.yanksing.com.*

This dim sum palace wins raves for the seemingly endless array of tasty offerings that tempt diners from its rolling carts. From Cantonese spring rolls to
house-roasted Peking duck to steamed shrimp dumplings and fried won tons
stuffed with curried shrimp and cream cheese, you'll be hard-pressed to
choose. Be forewarned if your eyes are bigger than your stomach:
dim sum items are priced a la carte—the more you eat, the more you'll pay.

Molinari Delicatessen $ Italian

*373 Columbus Ave., North Beach. Closed Sun & major holidays. 415-421-2337.
www.molinarideli.com.*

Heady whiffs of provolone, salami and olives waft from this century-old North
Beach institution. Locals pop in early to pick up handmade ravioli, tortellini,
olive oils and vinegars imported from Italy. Later in the morning, meats and
cheeses appear on the chopping block to feed the lunch crowd. Stop in for a
North Beach Special (prosciutto, provolone, sun-dried tomatoes and sweet bell
peppers) and picnic in Washington Square.

Dining in the Wine Country

French Laundry $$$$ French

6640 Washington St., Yountville. Dinner daily; lunch Fri, Sat & Sun. 707-944-2380. www.frenchlaundry.com.

Lodged in an unassuming century-old stone laundry building, the French Laundry was declared the "best restaurant in the world" in 2003 by *Restaurant Magazine*. Chef Thomas Keller, masterful in the preparation of sophisticated and creative French cuisine, offers three different prix-fixe dinners nightly: a five-course menu *($115)*, a nine-course chef's tasting menu *($135)*, and a nine-course vegetarian tasting menu *($115)*. A sommelier matches wines on request. Save your pennies and splurge for a special occasion—just be sure to make reservations two months in advance.

Tra Vigne $$$$ Italian

1050 Charter Oak Ave., St. Helena. Closed Mon. 707-963-4444. www.travignerestaurant.com.

Italian for "among the vines," Tra Vigne reflects founder Michael Chiarello's desire to bring southern Italy to northern California. Depending on the season, the menu might offer garlic-roasted Dungeness crab; half-moon-shaped pasta filled with butternut squash, roasted chanterelles and sage; and braised Niman Ranch short ribs with garlic polenta. The grand dining room boasts 30ft ceilings and huge windows. Stop in the adjacent gourmet shop, **Cantinetta**, for a glass of wine (they have more than 100 selections by the glass) and relax in the brick courtyard, shaded by mulberry trees.

Bistro Jeanty $$$ French

6510 Washington St., Yountville. 707-944-0103. www.bistrojeanty.com.

This charming neighborhood bistro on the main street in tiny Yountville is the brainchild of chef Philippe Jeanty, formerly of Domaine Chandon. Classics like *daube de boeuf* (beef stew with mashed potatoes, peas and carrots), *cassoulet* (a hearty stew of duck confit, white beans, sausage and bacon) and *moules au vin rouge* (mussels steamed in red wine) will linger in your memory long after they've disappeared from your plate. If you can't get reservations, walk-ins can sit at the communal table near the bar.

Cafe La Haye $$$ California-Mediterranean

140 E. Napa St., Sonoma. Dinner only. 707-935-5994. www.sterba.com/sonoma/lahaye.

Some big flavors come out of the tiny kitchen in this bistro just off Sonoma Plaza. Fresh produce, meats and cheeses from Sonoma and Napa valleys provide the ingredients for dishes such as house-smoked salmon with crisp potato-scallion pancakes and pan-roasted chicken breast with Laura Chenel goat cheese and herb stuffing. The wine list features a good selection of local boutique wines and the dining room is decorated with work by local artists.

John Ash & Co. $$$ California

4330 Barnes Rd., in the Vintners Inn, Santa Rosa. 707-527-7687. www.vintnersinn.com.

Surrounded by vineyards at the secluded Vintners Inn, 4mi north of Santa Rosa, chef Jeffrey Madura blends fresh seasonal ingredients with his own enthusiasm to create entrées like Zinfandel-steamed mussels with tomatoes, herbs and garlic, and grilled filet of beef with port-wine sauce and grilled red onions finished with Point Reyes blue cheese. If you can't tear yourself away, you can always book one of the 44 luxurious rooms at the inn.

Mustard's Grill $$$ American

7399 St. Helena Hwy. (Rte. 29), Napa. 709-944-2424. www.mustardsgrill.com.

A long-standing Napa Valley favorite, this casual ranch-style restaurant draws winemakers and other wine industry VIPs for its fresh cuisine and a top-notch wine list. The menu ranges across American regional dishes with nods to Continental and Asian, from seared ahi tuna to barbecued baby back ribs. For starters order the sublimely thin and crispy onion rings with house-made ketchup.

Terra $$$ California

1345 Railroad Ave., St. Helena. Dinner only. Closed Tue. 707-963-8931. www.terrarestaurant.com.

Since Terra has no sign outside, you'll need to recognize the restaurant by its building—a lovely 1884 fieldstone foundry with arched windows and doors. Inside the intimate dining room, you'll feel romantic amid soft lighting, stone walls and warm terra-cotta floors. Chef and owner Hiro Sone crafts innovative dishes using European and Asian influences: broiled sake-marinated Alaskan black cod, foie gras tortelloni, daube of lamb shoulder with Castroville artichokes. Sone's wife, pastry chef Lissa Doumani, does wonders with the likes of tiramisu, apple almond tart and chocolate bread pudding with sun-dried cherries and crème fraiche.

Tuscany $$ Italian

1005 First St., Napa. Dinner only. 707-258-1000. www.restaurant.com/tuscany.

Diners who can't get a table at Tra Vigne are delighted to find Tuscany in the bustling heart of Napa. The 1855 structure has been renovated with an open kitchen, where diners can watch braised Sonoma duck breast, rotisserie rabbit wrapped in pancetta, and other tempting dishes being prepared. Tiramisu or cannoli topped with warm peach compote makes a memorable end to a meal here.

Must Stay: San Francisco Hotels

The properties listed below were selected for their ambience, location and/or value for money. Prices reflect the average cost for a standard double room for two people (not including applicable city or state taxes). Hotels in San Francisco constantly offer special discount packages. Price ranges quoted do not reflect the California hotel tax of 14%. Properties are located in San Francisco, unless otherwise specified.

$$$$$	**over $300**	**$$**	**$75–$125**
$$$$	**$200–$300**	**$**	**less than $75**
$$$	**$125–$200**		

Luxury

Campton Place Hotel $$$$$ 110 rooms

340 Stockton St., Union Square. 415-781-5555 or 800-235-4300. www.camptonplace.com.

An intimate hotel popular in a former incarnation with the white-gloved "carriage trade" set, Campton Place is the epitome of elegance and fine service. Pear wood paneling and cozy window seats make up elements of the peaceful Asian-inspired room decor, while insulated glass filters out noise from nearby Union Square. Splurge on vibrant Mediterranean cuisine at **Campton Place Restaurant ($$$$)**— you can work it off later at the 9th-floor fitness center.

The Fairmont San Francisco $$$$$ 591 rooms

950 Mason St., Nob Hill. 415-772-5000 or 800-441-1414. www.fairmont.com.

This famous grand hotel atop Nob Hill survived the 1906 quake and saw the creation of the United Nations in 1945. The Fairmont's location at the intersection of San Francisco's two cable-car lines provides easy access to sightseeing. Choose from handsome rooms—renovated with new fabrics and furnishings in 2001—in the original building or in a 1961 tower that offers broad views across the city. The domed **Laurel Court** restaurant **($$$)** serves regional California fare. Don't miss happy hour at the exotic **Tonga Room and Hurricane Bar** with its thatched umbrellas and floating live band *(see Nightlife)*.

Four Seasons San Francisco $$$$$ 277 rooms

757 Market St., SoMa. 415-633-3000 or 800-819-5053. www.fourseasons.com.

Soft music and fine art envelop you as you step into the lobby of this South of Market newcomer. With a great location in the Yerba Buena Arts District one block from the cable-car turn-around on Powell Street, and two blocks from Union Square, the Four Seasons pampers guests in spacious rooms with floor-to-ceiling windows, thick terry robes and down pillows. Hotel guests have free access to the adjacent **Sports Club/LA**, with its 10,000sq ft gym, junior Olympic-size pool and full spa.

The Huntington Hotel $$$$$ 135 rooms

1075 California St., Nob Hill. 415-474-5400 or 800-227-4683. www.huntingtonhotel.com.

Overlooking Huntington Park on the California Street cable-car line, this 1924 classic started out as a luxury apartment complex. True to their origins, rooms are oversized and posh—think silk, damask, leather and velvet—fitting lodgings for the likes of former guests Luciano Pavarotti, Desmond Tutu and Paloma Picasso. Your palate will delight in New American dishes at the clubby **Big 4 Restaurant ($$$)**, and your stress will melt away after a treatment at the hotel's state-of-the-art **Nob Hill Spa** *(see Must Be Pampered)*.

Mandarin Oriental, San Francisco $$$$$ 158 rooms

222 Sansome St., Financial District. 415-276-9888 or 800-622-0404.
www.mandarin-oriental.com.

From the hotel's ground-floor entry, high-speed elevators whisk guests to their aeries, located between the 38th and 48th stories atop 345 California Center. Spectacular picture-window views await you in your room (binoculars provided), along with Egyptian cotton sheets, CD players and your choice of cotton or terrycloth robes and slippers. If trekking up San Francisco's hills isn't enough exercise for you, try a workout in the hotel's fitness center.

The Argent Hotel $$$$ 667 rooms

50 Third St., SoMa. 415-974-6400 or 877-222-6699. www.argenthotel.com.

Towering 36 stories above Yerba Buena Gardens at the heart of the city's dynamic new cultural district, this stylish, contemporary hotel boasts marble floors, rich woodwork, golf-leaf trim and a museum-class art collection on display throughout the hotel. The second-floor business center, full-size desks in the guest rooms and its location near the Moscone Convention Center make the Argent a good choice for business travelers. In the rooms, floor-to-ceiling windows look out over the stunning skyline.

Hotel Monaco $$$$ 201 rooms

501 Geary St., Theater District. 415-292-0100 or 866-622-5284. www.monaco-sf.com.

This 1910 Beaux-Arts classic offers high-style comfort in a convenient location a few blocks from Union Square. Baroque-style plaster fireplaces and sumptuous armchairs invite lobby conversation. In the guest rooms, Provençal fabrics drape over canopy beds and Chinese-inspired furnishings lend an exotic look. Housed in the former ballroom, now restored with Art Deco details, the stunning **Grand Café ($$$)** offers bistro-style meals. Your four-legged friends are welcome here, but if you can't bring Fido, ask for a goldfish to keep you company.

Hotel Palomar $$$$ 214 rooms

12 Fourth St., SoMa. 415-348-1111 or 866-373-4941. www.hotelpalomar.com.

The Kimpton Group's top-of-the-line venture embraces the fifth through ninth floors of a post-quake, 1908 landmark building at the corner of Market Street. Tailored lines, dramatic lighting and the hotel's signature leopard-print carpeting offer contemporary elegance throughout. Guests have access to complimentary car service to the Financial District and in-room spa services. The acclaimed **Fifth Floor** restaurant (**$$$$**) serves some of the city's best New French cuisine *(see Must Eat)*.

Westin St. Francis $$$$ 1,195 rooms

335 Powell St., Union Square. 415-397-7000 or 800-917-7458. www.westinstfrancis.com. See Landmarks.

Occupying a Renaissance- and Baroque-revival structure built in 1904, this landmark hotel facing Union Square is renowned for its legendary service. A historic charm still pervades the rooms in the main building with their Empire-style furnishings; more contemporary rooms with large bay windows and dramatic city views occupy the 32-story tower built in 1972. All are outfitted with Westin's signature Heavenly Bed™. At night, **The Compass Rose** tea salon becomes a lounge, with live entertainment and the hotel's signature frozen vodka martinis.

Moderate

Commodore Hotel
$$$ 110 rooms

825 Sutter St., Union Square. 415-923-6800 or 800-338-6848.
www.thecommodorehotel.com.

Hippest of the hip Joie de Vivre group, the Commodore is an offbeat urban oasis of neo-Deco styling. Whimsical custom furnishings, 1920s luxury-liner detailing and dramatic murals create an air of the unexpected. The colorful diner-like Titanic Café serves breakfast and lunch; the hypnotic Red Room lounge (it really *is* completely red!) stays open late for martini lovers.

Executive Hotel Vintage Court
$$$ 107 rooms

650 Bush St., Union Square. 415-392-4666 or 800-654-1100. www.vintagecourt.com.

This Euro-style property creates a cozy atmosphere in its lobby, where guests gather around the fireplace each evening to sample Napa Valley wines. Newly renovated in a palette of soft greens and cream, rooms invite relaxation with fluffy duvets and down pillows. Room rates hover at the lower end of the price range *($199-$229)*, making the Vintage Court a good choice for the price. Adjacent to the hotel, **Masa's ($$$$)** constantly wins raves for its contemporary French cuisine *(see Must Eat)*.

The Handlery Union Square Hotel
$$$ 377 rooms

351 Geary St., Union Square. 415-781-7800 or 800-843-4343. www.handlery.com.

A three-generation family operation that opened in 1948 (on the site of a 1907 hotel), The Handlery is a gracious inn, centrally located on Union Square. Rooms have been newly decorated with honey-colored woods, custom fabrics and Web TV. Perhaps the property's most noteworthy feature, the heated outdoor swimming pool and sauna are mid-city rarities.

Hotel Bohème
$$$ 15 rooms

444 Columbus Ave., North Beach. 415-433-9111. www.hotelboheme.com.

Reflecting the bohemian tastes of the Beat Generation in 1950s San Francisco, this quaint boutique hotel at the foot of Telegraph Hill is dedicated to the spirit of Jack Kerouac, Lawrence Ferlinghetti and their cohorts. Cozy rooms with burnt orange walls occupy a three-story building erected in the 1880s. The courteous staff is glad to help make reservations for restaurants, theater and tours.

Hotel Diva

$$$ 111 rooms

440 Geary St., Union Square. 415-885-0200 or 800-553-1900. www.personalityhotels.com.

The glitziest of several moderately priced San Francisco hotels in the Personality Hotels group, the trend-setting Diva is a polished Euro-tech inn, dramatically renovated in 1999 in the manner of an Art Deco-era ocean liner. Located in the Theater District, and popular with visiting members of the film industry, the property offers sleek contemporary rooms accented with black granite, stainless steel and cobalt-blue carpeting. Amenities include in-room CD players, a workout room and a video library.

Hotel Juliana

$$$ 107 rooms

590 Bush St., Nob Hill. 415-392-2540 or 866-325-9457. www.julianahotel.com.

Bold, bright and stylish in its decor, this nine-story boutique property at the foot of Nob Hill retains an intimate atmosphere in a 1903 building. The hotel packs in a lot of extras for the price: pillowtop beds, Aveda toiletries, a complimentary wine reception each evening, and weekday morning sedan service to the Financial District. There's a workout facility on-site, and your four-legged friends are welcome here.

Hotel Rex

$$$ 94 rooms

562 Sutter St., Union Square. 415-433-4434 or 800-433-4434. www.thehotelrex.com.

The redesign of this historic boutique hotel follows the theme of the literary and arts salons rife in San Francisco in the 1920s and 30s. Quotes from regional authors adorn the walls of different floors, including the hotel's Café Andrée. Sunny colors brighten the guest rooms, which are accented with hand-painted lampshades. With its dark paneling, comfortable seating and shelves of antiquarian books, the Rex's lobby has the feel of a gentleman's study.

Hotel Triton

$$$ 140 rooms

342 Grant Ave., Chinatown. 415-394-0500 or 800-800-1299. www.hoteltriton.com.

Standard fare certainly doesn't apply at this avant-garde boutique hotel facing Chinatown Gate, where the eye-popping room decor was designed by a group of local artists. With lodgings like Eco Rooms (all-natural linens, biodegradable toiletries), Zen Dens (feng shui incense, the Book of Buddha) and suites dedicated to rockers Jerry Garcia and Carlos Santana, you know it's got to be cutting-edge.  Custom armoires hide Sony flat-screen TVs, which, of course, include the 24-hour Yoga channel. All this and they're pet-friendly, too.

The Inn at the Opera $$$ 46 rooms

333 Fulton St., Civic Center. 415-863-8400 or 800-590-0157. www.innattheopera.com.

This elegant small hotel is popular among musicians and stage performers, owing to its location a block from the War Memorial Opera House (the stars often choose the Symphony or Opera suites). Tastefully decorated rooms include refrigerators, wet bar areas and microwaves for après-theater snacking. Intimate and romantic, the delightful **Ovation ($$$)** restaurant serves traditional French fare.

The Maxwell Hotel $$$ 153 rooms

386 Geary St., Union Square. 415-986-2000 or 888-734-6299. www.maxwellhotel.com.

Guest rooms in this chic boutique hotel, built in 1908 but restored in Art Deco style, reflect its Theater District setting in their stylish furnishings. Amenities focus on the hotel's proximity to upscale shopping: a shopping newsletter, department-store coupons and a Maxwell Hotel shopping bag in every cheerful room. The Maxwell even offers gift-wrapping services. New York deli-style fare is available from Max's on the Square restaurant (**$$$**).

The Palace Hotel $$$ 552 rooms

2 New Montgomery St., Financial District. 415-512-1111 or 800-325-3589.
www.sfpalace.com.

A Market Street landmark since 1875, The Palace—now a Starwood hotel—bridges the gap between the 19C and the 21C. Renovated from head to toe in 1991, the Palace shines again with its centerpiece, the sumptuous **Garden Court** Decked out with marble pillars, stained-glass domed ceiling and Austrian crystal chandeliers, the Garden Court has hosted many a VIP event over the years. Luxurious rooms, newly updated in tones of soft blue, cream and yellow, are appointed with 14ft ceilings, marble baths, down comforters and windows that open. The on-site spa features a heated indoor lap pool.

Sir Francis Drake Hotel $$$ 417 rooms

450 Powell St., Union Square. 415-392-7755 or 800-795-7129. www.sirfrancisdrake.com.

Named for the English explorer who sailed into the area in 1579, the Drake was the city's most opulent luxury hotel when it opened in 1928. That air of grandeur still rules today, evident in the doorman in Beefeater costume and in the sumptuous lobby, with its marble staircase, crystal chandeliers and gold-leaf ceiling. Resting on the cable-car line one block from Union Square, the hotel's 21st-floor penthouse holds one of San Francisco's most popular nightclubs, **Harry Denton's Starlight Room** *(see Nightlife).*

Stanyan Park Hotel
$$$ 36 rooms

750 Stanyan St., Haight-Ashbury. 415-741-1000.
www.stanyanpark.com.

Overlooking Golden Gate Park on the west end of bohe-mian Haight Street, this three-story 1905 Victorian house rates inclusion on the National Register of Historic Places. Tasteful rooms, all refurbished in 2001, are decorated with period furnishings—Victorian, of course—and fea-ture sitting areas, color TVs and full baths. Reasonable rates include continental breakfast and afternoon tea.

Washington Square Inn
$$$ 15 rooms

1660 Stockton St., North Beach. 415-981-4220 or 800-388-0220. www.wsisf.com.

A charming and intimate European-style inn at the foot of Telegraph Hill in the heart of bohemian North Beach, this lovely bed-and-breakfast is proud of its highly personalized service. Individually decorated rooms feature French antiques, fresh orchids and robes; some have sitting area and fireplaces. Rates include afternoon tea, evening wine and hors-d'oeuvres, and a continental breakfast either delivered to your room or served downstairs at the antique table overlooking the square.

Budget

Andrews Hotel
$$ 48 rooms

624 Post St., Union Square. 415-563-6877 or 800-926-3739. www.andrewshotel.com.

This bright and cozy Victorian inn offers intimacy and personal service in the European style, three blocks off Union Square. Rooms sport pastel colors and floral prints and are equipped with small TVs and VCRs (complimentary movies are available at the front desk). Each morning, a complimentary continental break-fast—breads, seasonal fruits, coffee, tea—is delivered to the landing on each floor. In the evening, enjoy a glass of California wine—on the house—at Fino restaurant.

Chancellor Hotel
$$ 137 rooms

433 Powell St., Union Square. 415-362-2004 or 800-428-4748. www.chancellorhotel.com.

Location is everything at this European-style 15-story inn, opened in 1914 on the Powell-Hyde and Powell-Mason cable-car lines, right on Union Square. One of the city's best bargains, the Chancellor boasts amenities like in-room safes, a pillow menu (choose your favorite style), and an on-site restaurant (Luques), that you'd expect from a higher-priced property. Guests have free access to the health club at the Westin St. Francis, a mere half-block away.

Grant Plaza Hotel
$$ 72 rooms

465 Grant Ave., Chinatown. 415-434-3883 or 800-472-6899. www.grantplaza.com.

A remarkable value in the heart of Chinatown, this clean, bright inn may be simple, but it offers such modern conveniences as data ports, hair dryers and electronic key cards. Rooms have color TVs and newly renovated private baths. The cable car to Fisherman's Wharf is just a block away, and Union Square shopping is an easy three-block walk away from the hotel.

Hotel Beresford $$ 114 rooms

635 Sutter St., Union Square. 415-673-9900 or 800-533-6533.
http://beresford.citysearch.com.

This pleasant, family-run hotel attracts British visitors with its Victorian decor and its English pub, the White Horse Tavern. Rooms are small, but nicely furnished in dark woods and pastels. Rates include a basic continental breakfast. The property's similarly priced sister hotel, the **Hotel Beresford Arms** *(701 Post St.; 415-673-2600; 102 rooms),* is three blocks away.

Hotel Bijou $$ 65 rooms

111 Mason St., Union Square. 415-771-1200 or 800-771-1022. www.hotelbijou.com.

Located a block away from cable-car stops, the Art Deco-style Bijou recalls a 1920s movie palace; on its walls hang photos of San Francisco's old movie houses. Bright, jewel-toned guest rooms are named for films shot in the city, which are illustrated in each room by original still photographs. Double features of San Francisco-based films are screened nightly in the small lobby theater. Rates include a complimentary continental breakfast.

Nob Hill Hotel $$ 50 rooms

835 Hyde St., Nob Hill. 415-885-2987 or 877-662-4455. www.nobhillhotel.com.

Restored in 1998, this neighborhood gem—which dates from 1906—has reclaimed its original marble flooring, alabaster chandeliers and stained-glass windows. Cozy rooms sport Victorian furnishings and objets d'art, iron beds and velvet comforters, along with mini refrigerators, microwaves and coffee makers. The hotel's **Ristorante Il Cartoccio ($$$)** specializes in Italian cuisine.

San Remo Hotel $ 62 rooms

2237 Mason St., North Beach. 415-776-8688 or 800-352-7366. www.sanremohotel.com.

Simplicity rules here: like a European pension, all rooms in the San Remo share baths, and none have phones or TVs. Cozy accommodations are neatly kept and pretty, furnished with late-19C antiques. Ask the friendly, helpful staff to direct you to popular sights, such as Fisherman's Wharf, which lie within easy walking distance.

Luxury

Auberge du Soleil
$$$$$ 50 rooms

180 Rutherford Hill Rd., Rutherford. 707-963-1211 or 800-348-5406. www.aubergedusoleil.com.

The breezy terrace of this upscale country inn offers the wine-weary traveler an unparalleled view across the Napa Valley. Accommodations consist mainly of one- and two-bedroom suites tucked into the hillside overlooking the 33 acres of silvery olive trees that surround the property. While you're here, sample Mediterranean-inspired cuisine at the

Restaurant at Auberge du Soleil ($$$$), and pamper yourself with a Napa-themed treatment at the **Spa du Soleil** *(see Must Be Pampered).*

Meadowood Napa Valley
$$$$$ 99 rooms

900 Meadowood Lane, St. Helena. 707-963-3646 or 800-458-8080. www.meadowood.com.

A perfect perch for Wine Country adventures, this world-class resort off Napa's Silverado Trail offers top-flight service. Exquisite grounds encompass rustic cottages set in a wooded grove; rooms feature private terraces and stone fireplaces. Between golf, tennis, the full-service spa (offering Ayurvedic treatments and therapeutic Yoga), and the wine center (whose staff can arrange tastings and vineyard picnics), it would be easy never to leave the property. Don't miss innovative Wine Country cuisine at the superb **Restaurant at Meadowood ($$$$)**.

Fairmont Sonoma Mission Inn & Spa
$$$$ 230 rooms

18140 Sonoma Hwy. (Rte. 12), Boyes Hot Springs. 707-938-9000 or 800-257-7544. www.sonomamissioninn.com.

This early-20C resort just outside the town of Sonoma achieved fame long before spas became endemic. Inside pink stucco walls and Mission-style architecture, every modern touch prevails, from high-tech phones to aromatherapy wraps. Rooms in the historic main building, decorated with pine furnishings, ceiling fans and plantation shutters, were restored in early 2004. The grounds include an 18-hole golf course, and the spa *(see Must Be Pampered)* boasts its own on-site source of thermal mineral water. **Santé ($$$)** is renowned for its California cuisine.

Honor Mansion
$$$$ 14 rooms

14891 Grove St., Healdsburg. 707-433-4277 or 800-554-4667. www.honormansion.com.

Luxury awaits you behind the door of this restored 1883 house, where owners Cathi and Steve Fowler have anticipated their guests' nearly every need in individually decorated rooms and suites. Four lovely vineyard suites out back spell romance with gas fireplaces and private patios with your own outdoor whirlpool. Rates (rooms start at $180) include a rich multicourse breakfast that will prepare you for a long day of wine tasting. Ask the helpful staff to arrange for wine tours or to pack you a picnic lunch.

Villagio Inn & Spa $$$$ 112 rooms

6481 Washington St., Yountville. 707-944-8877 or 800-351-1133. www.villagio.com.

Reminiscent of a Tuscan village—with two-story villas surrounding lush gardens and vineyards, fountains and waterways, swimming pools and tennis courts—the Villagio combines its resort atmosphere with a health spa *(see Must Be Pampered)*. In the rooms, warm tones are accented by wood-burning fireplaces. Rates include a welcome bottle of wine, a champagne continental breakfast  and afternoon tea. Villagio's older sister, the lovely **Vintage Inn ($$$$)**, is right up the street *(6541 Washington St.; 707-944-1112 or 800-351-1133; www.vintageinn.com)*.

Moderate

El Bonita Motel $$$ 41 rooms

195 Main St., St. Helena. 707-963-3216 or 800-541-3284. www.elbonita.com.

Located in the heart of the delightful town of St. Helena, this roadside motel offers clean, comfortable rooms decked out with such conveniences as kitchenettes, irons and ironing boards and hairdryers; some rooms even have whirlpool baths. Stroll the gardens or take a dip in the swimming pool. If weather permits, you can enjoy your complimentary continental breakfast outside on the patio.

Sonoma Hotel $$$ 16 rooms

110 W. Spain St., Sonoma. 707-996-2996 or 800-468-6016. www.sonomahotel.com.

From the stone fireplace in the lobby to the claw-foot tubs, twig nightstands and rustic iron headboards in the cozy guest rooms, this hotel oozes country charm. It was built in 1880 on the northwest corner of Sonoma's town square as a dry-goods store and community center. Guests are treated to a continental breakfast each morning and a wine tasting in the lobby each evening. The hotel's restaurant, **the girl & the fig ($$$)**, characterizes its fine fare as "country food with a French passion." The late-night brasserie menu **($$)** is available until 11pm.

Hotel La Rose $$ 49 rooms

308 Wilson St., Santa Rosa. 707-579-3200 or 800-527-6738. www.hotellarose.com.

Rooms in the original stone structure (1907), on Railroad Square in the heart of Santa Rosa's historic district, are individually outfitted with American and European antiques as well as modern amenities such as large-screen TVs. Ask for a room in the newer Carriage House across the street; second-floor rooms here have 15ft peaked windows and French doors opening onto balconies that overlook a garden courtyard. A complimentary continental breakfast, served in the main inn's cheery breakfast room, includes fresh-squeezed orange juice and coffee roasted on the premises.

Index

The following abbreviations may appear in this Index: NHP National Historic Park; NHS National Historic Site; NRA National Recreation Area; SHP State Historic Park; SP State Park.

124   MICHELIN MUST SEES

Index

Photo Credits:

YOUR OPINION MATTERS!

Thank you for purchasing a Michelin Travel Publications' product. To help us continue to offer you the absolute best in travel guides, maps and atlases, we need your feedback.

Please fill in this questionnaire and return it to:
Michelin Travel Publications – Attn: Marketing
P.O. Box 19001
Greenville, SC 29602-9001, USA

To thank you, we will draw one name from the returned questionnaires each month from May 2004 to year end. Each month's winner will receive a free 2004 North America Road Atlas, or a set of the Must SEES travel guides, or a set of the Regional Road Atlas + Travel Guides.

1. How would you rate the following features of the product, if applicable?

1 = *Very Good*   **2** = *Acceptable*   **3** = *Poor*

	1	2	3
Selection of attractions/sights	❏	❏	❏
Practical Information (prices, etc.)	❏	❏	❏
Description of establishments	❏	❏	❏
General presentation	❏	❏	❏
Cover	❏	❏	❏

2. How satisfied were you with this product?

❏ Very satisfied   ❏ Satisfied   ❏ Somewhat Satisfied   ❏ Not Satisfied

If not satisfied, how should we improve the product? _____

_____

3. Did you buy this product: *(check all that apply)*
❏ For holiday/vacation
❏ For short breaks or weekends
❏ For business purposes
❏ As a gift
❏ Other

4. Where would you buy and expect our products to be available?
(check all that apply)

❏ Supermarket   ❏ Mass Merchandiser (Costco, Sam's, etc.)
❏ Convenience store   ❏ Specialty store (museum shop, travel store, etc.)
❏ Bookstore   ❏ Gas/Service Station
❏ Online   ❏ Kiosk/Gift shop

5. Which destinations do you visit the most often for pleasure? *(list as many locations as you wish)* _____

_____

Tear Here

MSSF04

6. Which destinations do you visit the most often for business? *(list as many locations as you wish)* _____

_____

7. When you go on vacation, generally how long do you stay?
(check all that apply)
❏ Three or four days
❏ One week
❏ Two weeks
❏ A combination of short (three or four days) and one week vacations
❏ Other _____

8. When you travel, what mode of transportation do you most frequently use?
(1 – most frequent, 6 – least frequent)
_____Plane _____Car _____Bus _____Train _____Cruise _____Other

9. Would you consider buying other Michelin travel books or products?
❏ Yes   ❏ No
If yes, which one(s):
❏ Must SEES
❏ North America 2004 Road Atlas
❏ North America Regional Road Atlas + Travel Guide
❏ North America Regional Road Atlas
❏ North America Regional Maps
❏ Green Guide (North American titles)
❏ Green Guide (European titles)
❏ Red Guide
❏ European City Maps
❏ Other_____

10. Your age?
❏ Less than 25 years old   ❏ 25–35 years old   ❏ 36–45 years old
❏ 46–55 years old   ❏ 56–65 years old   ❏ 65 years plus

11. Additional Comments:

_____

_____

Telephone or e-mail where we may reach you: _____
If you would like to be added to our mailing list, please fill out the information below:
❏ Ms.   ❏ Mrs.   ❏ Mr.
Name _____
Address _____
City_____ State _____
Zip Code_____ Country_____
E-mail (optional): _____

Tear Here